Raves for
I've Still Got It . . .

"Jenna McCarthy's *I've Still Got It . . .* is everything you could want in a book *or* a best friend—blunt, truthful, and dead-on hilarious. Her unflinching look at the vagaries of middle age is witty and astute and will give you comfort in knowing that you're not the only person whose arms are suddenly too short to read the menu. Granted, you'll still have your laugh lines after reading this, but at least you'll have earned them. More than ever, Jenna McCarthy proves that 'she's still got it' in this hysterical collection!"

—Jen Lancaster, *New York Times* bestselling author of
Bitter Is the New Black and *The Tao of Martha*

"Hilarious and spot-on! Jenna McCarthy's *I've Still Got It . . .* made me howl. Her comic timing and quirky wisdom have never been better!"

—Celia Rivenbark, *New York Times* bestselling author of
Rude Bitches Make Me Tired

"Jenna McCarthy is Lena Dunham if she had kids and shopped at Costco, or Howard Stern if he had prettier hair and a thing for happy hour. In *I've Still Got It . . .* , she spins wildly entertaining essays from the simplest themes, from domestic clutter to the realities of aging and her (increasingly) sagging body parts. With whip-smart humor, older-sister warmth, and wickedly sharp insight, Jenna proves she's been there, done that . . . and bought all the sparkly things at Target because they were on sale, damn it! I loved every word of this delightful, relatable book and I think you will, too."

—Anna Goldfarb, author of *Clearly, I Didn't Think This Through*

continued . . .

continued . . .

"Every relationship is like being fit, healthy, and happy—you have to work at it. Jenna reminds us of this with wit, insight, and self-deprecating humor. At the end of the day, you'll recognize yourself in these pages and applaud her honesty."

—Lucy Danziger, editor-in-chief of
Self magazine and coauthor of *The Nine Rooms of Happiness*

"An uproariously funny, deliciously satisfying, and completely accurate take on wedded bliss."

—Tracy Beckerman, syndicated humor columnist and author of
Lost in Suburbia

"When Jenna McCarthy turns her wicked wit to the, ahem, challenges of modern-day marriage, hilarity ensues. Anyone still in love with the oaf they married will find a lot to love here."

—Julie Tilsner, author of *29 and Counting:
A Chick's Guide to Turning 30*

"This should be required reading for all brides. No, make that required reading for any woman who has been snookered into believing that finding and marrying the right person will somehow catapult her into a fairy tale—complete with a snorting horse, castle, and prince. With humor and insight, Jenna takes us on an enlightening tour of the true realities of marriage, and she amazingly pulls off the impossible: She helps us to fall in love with our farting, nose-picking, burping, sex-obsessed doofus husbands all over again."

—Alisa Bowman, *New York Times* bestselling
coauthor of *The Skinny*

I've Still Got It

. . . I Just Can't Remember Where I Put It

AWKWARDLY TRUE TALES
FROM THE FAR SIDE OF FORTY

JENNA McCARTHY

BERKLEY BOOKS, NEW YORK

THE BERKLEY PUBLISHING GROUP
Published by the Penguin Group
Penguin Group (USA) LLC
375 Hudson Street, New York, New York 10014

USA • Canada • UK • Ireland • Australia • New Zealand • India • South Africa • China

penguin.com

A Penguin Random House Company

This book is an original publication of The Berkley Publishing Group.

Library of Congress Cataloging-in-Publication Data
McCarthy, Jenna.
I've still got it, I just can't remember where I put it : awkwardly true tales from the far side of
forty / Jenna McCarthy—Berkley trade paperback edition.
pages cm
ISBN 978-0-425-27253-4
1. Middle age—Humor.   2. Middle-aged women—Humor.   I. Title.
PN6231. M47 M365 2014
818'.602 —dc23
2014000555

PUBLISHING HISTORY
Berkley trade paperback edition / July 2014

PRINTED IN THE UNITED STATES OF AMERICA

10 9 8 7 6 5 4 3 2 1

Cover photograph by Getty Images / Cultura.
Cover design by George Long.

For Sophie and Sasha.

*Even though you give me gray hair and
ask me what it was like being alive in the 1900s
and tell me that you've figured out why my butt is so flat
("Because you sit on it all day!"), you make me laugh,
and that keeps me young. I love you with
every fiber in my wrinkled being.*

I wasn't going to write this page at all.

For one thing, you may have heard some grumbling recently about a few authors going a teensy bit overboard in their acknowledgments ("I'd like to thank Vladimir Putin for helping me pick out the exquisite, supple, ridiculously overpriced lambskin leather chair I sat on each day whilst Skypeing with the Dalai Lama and channeling this book . . . "), and I certainly wouldn't want to be one of them.

And also, even though I'm supported by an impossibly amazing team of people in both my personal and professional lives, I pretty much wrote what you're about to read all by myself.

[Pats self on the back. "Thanks for not quitting halfway through, self. Without you, this book would really suck."]

That said, if I'm going to thank anybody, I would have to start with my ass-kicking agent, Laurie Abkemeier, for believing in me and my potty mouth from the get-go and also consistently helping me put food on my table. My kids are *really* whiny when they're hungry, so it would be hard to overstate my gratitude here.

I also humbly bow to my too-lovely-to-be-true Berkley editor, Denise Silvestro, who tells me she's easy on me because I'm "just a pro," even though I secretly think it's because she's afraid of me. Writing for you is like sucking down that first mango margarita on Cinco de Mayo: pure, unadulterated joy.

To the badass writers whose names are shamelessly plastered on this book in the hopes that someone, somewhere might see one of them and go, "Holy shit! If *s/he* likes it I'm buying thirteen copies!!!" I hope (for your sake, of course) one day I am so goddamned famous that you're shocked that I have the time and grace to return the favor. Which I totally will. Swear.

Finally, to every pair of hands I've never even had the pleasure of shaking that designed, proofread, copyedited, scanned this book for liabilities or otherwise kept me from getting sued or looking like an ass: If you're ever in Santa Barbara, look me up. Mango margaritas are on me!

Oh, fine. And to my inner circle of family and friends (you know who you are, and if you're going "I might be?" then you're not) for being totally batshit crazy. I'm told that if you weren't, I wouldn't be funny. So please don't ever change. I have a lot more books to write.

CONTENTS

Contents

May Contain Nuts

Having written several books before this one, let's just say this is not my first rodeo. Thanks to passionate reader feedback I now know that some people are offended by profanity, vanity, whining, wealth, dog bashing, truth telling, and anything resembling a heteronormative (I had to look it up the first time, too) perspective. They get mad when you admit that you grew up financially comfortable or you fail to include the LGBTQ point of view on a subject or you bitch about your husband— *in a marriage book*, for the love of all that is sacred. And *some people* get so mightily, huffily upset when they encounter these things in your book that they dash to their computers and call you an asshat on Amazon or write you a scathing email informing you that your very foul mouth is appalling. (In my defense, that was in reference to a book I wrote and *put a swear word right in the title*, so you'd think this angry lady might have had some idea what she was getting into before she cracked the spine. But apparently no.) So I just wanted to let you know up front that the book you are holding has all of the above and probably many, many more potentially offensive elements, including but not limited to an entire bit about my vagina. If you're like me, that just sealed your decision to buy or read it. (Not my vagina in particular, but you know what I mean.) If you're like the finger-wagger who called me and my trucker mouth unladylike—and by the way, name-calling is not a very ladylike thing to do, in my opinion—maybe you should get yourself a nice kitten calendar or Sudoku book instead.

You're Only as Old as Your Vagina

I was at dinner with a group of girlfriends when the conversation turned, as it frequently does these days, to cosmetic surgery. *But not the kind you're thinking about.* No, we weren't discussing brow lifts or butt implants or big, bouncy new boobs or even a little subtle liposculpting. The topic—and you might want to brace yourself for this one—was vaginal rejuvenation. And not in the "hey doc, while you're down there working your episiotomy magic, maybe you could throw in an extra stitch or two, wink, wink" sense, either. That actually would be considered reconstructive surgery, the mostly medically-necessary kind that's designed to improve a body part's particular function. Apparently there is something—a cosmetic procedure, an actual *thing*—that women are paying

God knows how many thousands of dollars for so that their lady parts will look . . . prettier. And younger. And even, dare I say it? Fresher.

"But what . . . ? Why . . . ?" I was not contributing very effectively to the conversation. First of all, I was too embarrassed to admit that I hadn't recently (or more accurately, ever) given my muffin anything resembling a thorough inspection, so I wasn't even sure if it looked old and ugly. But more importantly, *did it matter if it did*? I guess to some gals, it most certainly did.

According to one practitioner's website (because hell yeah, I Googled it), the cosmetic procedure in question—it's called a labiaplasty, by the way—"changes the size or shape of the labia, typically making them smaller or correcting an asymmetry between them." To be clear, I had absolutely no clue if my labia were oversized or lopsided, and I wasn't about to start caring. All I could think when I read this was: *Haven't we raised the bar high enough already, people? Now our fucking vaginas have to look twenty-two forever, too? Where will it end?*

I wondered about old women with youthful vaginas more than I should have. Were they porn stars or prostitutes or just lust-driven nymphomaniacs? Had some cruel lover given their beavers an unkind nickname that compelled these gals, in collective droves of despair, to long to be more beautiful . . . down there? Were they plastic surgery junkies who'd just about run out of body parts to perfect but then they caught a glimpse of their V-traps in a mirror and thought, *Whoops, I almost forgot about that!?* Because I'd have to be pretty damned pleased with every other inch of my body before it would even occur to me to mess with that particular part. "Let's see, my neck doesn't jiggle, my thighs are smooth and cellulite free, my rack is up around my neck . . . I'll just get a little labia trim and then I'll be good as new!"

I hadn't even recovered from the vagina business when I found myself having a life-changing conversation with my sister Laurie. I was relating something my doctor had said that Laurie, as a health professional, found surprising.

"How old is he?" Laurie wanted to know.

"He's young," I told her. "You know, our age."

Even though Laurie is an otherwise lovely person, she had the nerve to laugh at this.

"Jen, we are not young," she said.

It was one thing to learn that my vagina might be getting a little long in the tooth; it was another to hear—from my older sister—that *I* was.

"Well, we're not *old*," I said, a thirteen on your one-to-ten defensiveness scale. *Old* is a relative term of course, but I think it's safe to define it as "twenty or more years older than you are when being asked to define it."

"No, we're midlife," my bitch of a sister informed me cavalierly. I am forty-five, and Laurie is forty-seven. Were we past our best-by dates already? And if we were, when had that happened?

"Mom's midlife," I contended.

"No, Mom's old. *We're* midlife," Laurie insisted.

"Well, your vagina is older than mine," I spat.

Was it hot in there or was it just me?

I did not like that word, *midlife*. For one thing, it sounded like *midwife*, which immediately conjured images of childbirth, a process I found more than a little traumatizing. Plus it sort of implied that I was halfway to the grave, which surely couldn't be the case. The roadmap of lines on my face and my possibly withered vagina notwithstanding (I never did check*), I didn't feel one bit different than I did when I was twenty-five and staying up all night dancing on bar stools. Well, maybe a tad less energetic. And probably a little more impatient. And I guess slightly more edgy. And definitely more confident. And a lot more squishy and "I don't give a shit." But other than those things, exactly the same.

The other issue I was having was that everyone knows *midlife* isn't a noun; it's an adjective—created to modify a single word: *crisis*. "Midlife crisis," we whisper when we hear our friend Gina is having a fling with her gardener or Eve's getting an eye lift. We're half jealous (we want free hedge trims and perky eyes, too, damn it!), half relieved that we're not the ones experiencing what some might consider the equivalent of a grown-up temper tantrum.

I was almost definitely positive that I wasn't having any sort of crisis, but just to be sure, I Googled it. On the UK's *Daily Telegraph* website I found a handy list of "signs you're having a midlife crisis," and for the record, inspecting your vagina for signs of listlessness was *not* on the list. Here are a few items

---

* Fine, I checked. It was pretty ugly—but how would I know if it was uglier than anyone else's?

that were (note that some may be paraphrased because Brits love using fancy spelling for words like *realise* that my spell-check feature does not like):

1. Wishing for a simpler life. *[Stares at unread stack of* Real Simple *magazines in horror.]*

2. Looking up old flames on Facebook. *Crap.*

3. Compulsively reminiscing about your childhood. *But catching fireflies and riding a bike without a helmet, you guys! That shit was awesome.*

4. Obsessively comparing your appearance with your peers. *Define "obsessively" please,* Telegraph.

5. Discovering your hangovers are worse and last longer than they used to. *Not if you keep drinking!*

6. Revisiting vacation spots you went to as a child. *But I already know how to get there!*

7. Googling medical symptoms. *Do young people not do this???*

8. Tooling around town on a fancy new bike. *Whew! Dodged a bullet there.*

9. Taking up a new hobby. *Does searching online for plastic surgery before-and-after pictures count, do you suppose?*

10. Finding yourself easily distracted. *Wait, what was I saying?*

After I determined that at least by UK standards I had several of the symptoms of a classic midlife crisis, I proceeded to do something I generally try to avoid: I did some math. If I lived to be ninety, I would be squarely in the middle of my life. Even if I lived to ninety-five, I'd fall in the range. I'd pretty much have to reach a hundred and ten to even remotely be considered young by relative standards.

I'm not going to lie to you, my odds of living to a hundred and ten are slim. I grew up on a steady diet of Kraft macaroni and cheese and cream cheese and jelly on Wonder Bread sandwiches. When I wasn't cramming my piehole with such healthy, gourmet delights, I was very busy secondhand chain-smoking four packs of unfiltered Kool cigarettes a day. I did this religiously for the first eighteen years of my life, indulging on airplanes, in the car, and right at the kitchen table. Sometimes *during* dinner. I partied my ass off before, during, and after college.* I consume far more Chardonnay and cheeseburgers than the Surgeon General recommends, and I can count on one hand how many "good night's sleep" I get in a year. In other words, I'd be one lucky fucker if I were only halfway to the finish line here.

I probably don't need to point out that midlife isn't what it used to be, either. When my parents were my age, they were just kicking back and starting to enjoy the fruits of a lifetime

---

* I mean that literally. You should see my ass. I honestly don't have one. When I turn to the side, I look like SpongeBob SquarePants. I hear there's a procedure that can correct this.

of labor. They were empty nesters on the verge of retirement. They had fat bank accounts, their house was paid off, and their biggest annual stressor was deciding whether to take a beach vacation or a ski vacation or both. They owned a lake house and several boats, and had already put two kids through college. (Neither of them came from money, by the way, and Dad was a high school dropout. They just started young, busted their humps, and finished young.) My mom had a round tummy and droopy boobs and a furrow between her eyes but so did all of her friends, so none of them worried or even thought about these things much. Mom took ceramics classes and made homemade ice cream, and Dad spent long hours sanding the teak on his boats. They had free time pouring out of their ears. They may have been fulfilled or they may not have been, but they certainly weren't buying books on the subject or attending happiness seminars or wondering if their junk was young and fetching enough. If they felt any angst about being in this halfway place, they drowned it in whiskey tonics and went blindly about the business of life.

Compare their forties to, say, mine. I've just secured a fabulous new thirty-year loan that I hope (but occasionally doubt) I will live to see paid off. Most days I work from five a.m. to eight p.m., taking breaks to shop for healthy, organic, locally sourced groceries that can be prepared in fifteen minutes or less, squeeze in the occasional workout, organize the overabundance of crap that never stops parading into my house, wash endless loads of laundry, enjoy an occasional shag, and shuffle my kids to volleyball games and gymnastics classes and tennis practice and hip-hop performances—all while managing to check my email and text messages approximately every thirteen seconds. I take crappy writing assignments I don't want to so I can send my kids to summer camps—and not the chichi sleep-away kind, either; I'm talking regular old day camps. When my husband and I talk about retirement, it's almost always in the context of a "what we'd do if we won the lottery" conversation and hardly ever rooted in anything resembling reality. I watch my peers getting chemical peels and hair extensions and lip injections and tummy tucks, and I silently beg them to *just fucking stop* so that the playing field might be a little more level. I stand in the mirror a lot and do this thing where I tug my facial skin up and out toward my temples, and I smirk at the unlined but clownish facsimile of my younger self staring back at me. I still wear very short skirts with very high heels, but I do this knowing that it's not entirely appropriate. Fortunately, I don't give a shit.

I guess getting older does have its benefits.

CHAPTER 1

Aging Gracefully and Other Things I Know Nothing About

You can tell a lot about a woman by peering into her medicine cabinet. Unlatch that door, and you'll know immediately, for instance, if she is prone to cold sores or wears contact lenses or has trouble falling asleep. You'll recognize right away if she occasionally gets gas, pops allergy pills, or battles athlete's foot or yeast infections. And you can discern, with little uncertainty, just how desperate she is to stop the relentless march of time—the one that's hell-bent on leaving muddy footprints across her face before beelining straight down to her ankles.

If a burglar broke into my house, he'd be a fool to ignore my medicine cabinet. There's probably several hundred dollars' worth of lotions and potions in there, and each and every one is emblazoned with the word *ANTI-AGING* or something synonymous.

I've got products that promise to plump, refine, resurface, tighten, and tone; creams designed to minimize pores and dry up "adult acne" and fade age spots and, if all of those fail, hide the lot of them. The wrinkle fighters take up two deep shelves on their own. My shampoo and conditioner don't just fight age, they *defy* it, people; even my toothpaste guarantees a younger-looking smile (which is totally awesome because I can't think of anything hotter than a forty-five-year-old sporting braces).

Here's the worst part: If you added up the money I've spent stockpiling my anti-aging arsenal over the years, you could probably buy a brand-new Range Rover with it. Which really pisses me off, seeing as I am here to tell you *that shit did not work.* I like to cling to the vague possibility that without it, I'd look even older and more haggard, but unless I find I have a separated-at-birth twin out there who hasn't been indulging in these luxuries, it's not like there's any way to find out. Even with dutiful use of my overpriced haul, I have not-so-fine lines around my eyes, deep grooves on either side of my mouth, and a constellation of spots that may have something to do with my liver dotting the better part of my face.

This did not happen overnight. Although I worked hard on aging my skin all throughout adolescence and early adulthood (think: iodine-laced baby oil and monthly unlimited tanning bed memberships*), I'd say the visible decline started

---

* I kid you not: I was tanorexic. If you look at photos of me in my teens and twenties, all you see are teeth and the whites of my eyes. But don't worry; I'm paying for it now.

around thirty and has been steadily accelerating ever since. It's one of those things you don't really notice—like your kids getting taller or your house paint starting to fade and chip—until you stumble across a photo of what it used to look like. Every time I see a picture that was taken ten or seven or even two years ago, I have exactly the same thought: *Wow, I look so young.* This is when I do the skin-tugging thing—up and out until it's taut across my face—and marvel at the difference several months and a few millimeters makes.

There was a time in my life when I didn't think twice about having my picture taken. After all, pictures are just captured moments; what was there to think about? It turns out a lot—like lighting and shadows and angles,* to name a few. After a certain age, if all of those elements aren't perfectly aligned in your favor, you wind up looking like Ebenezer Scrooge or Nick Nolte in every shot.

It never fails. I'll get all decked out and done up and think I look pretty damned good, and then someone will whip out their iPhone and snap a picture, and I'm like, "Wow, who's that old lady who jumped in front of me right as you were clicking the—*OMG.*" Is my mirror broken? Do I need stronger glasses? Why do I look like a bloated corpse? Delete, delete, delete. I delete a *lot* of pictures. I realize that there's always

---

* Speaking of angles, *never* let a child take your picture unless you are both sitting nose to nose. Otherwise the view of your face from down there—ostensibly the view he sees all day every day but let's not dwell on that—is a ghastly stretch of jiggly, wrinkly, turkey-waddle neck skin.

Photoshop, but that's a double-edged sword because if you go around posting all of these doctored shots all over Facebook, when people see you in person, they're going wonder what the hell happened. It's a lose-lose.

Recently my literary agent wondered casually if I had a different headshot I'd like to use on my books and in my marketing materials. "You don't like the one I'm using?" I asked her, surprised. I loved that picture! What was wrong with her?

"Well, um, it's just . . ." she stammered. "When was that picture taken?"

"I think it was 2005 or 2006," I told her. "Why? Is that bad?"

"You might consider using a more recent one," she suggested gently.

Well, why would I go and do a thing like *that*? I knew I'd never take another picture that good again, because I'd never look that good again. Oh right, the in-person letdown. I mentioned this conversation weepily to my husband.

"You're still hot for your age," he insisted, as if this was consolation. To me this response sounded like "I'd still do you," which is fairly meaningless since I'm the only one he's got clear and reliable access to for those purposes.

Still, I was almost inclined to believe him until a recent shopping trip to Bed Bath & Beyond. I wandered into the magnifying mirror aisle where I made the mistake of peering into one of these tools of the devil. The one I chose, purely by accident, had a ring of fluorescent lightbulbs all around it and a sticker boasting MAGNIFIES TWELVE TIMES right on the glass.

In retrospect I should have known this would be a bad idea, after long-ago learning that the smaller I make my pictures, the better I look in them. (Postage-stamp size is ideal, but good luck finding frames.) But before I could stop to consider the wisdom of what I was doing, I pushed my nose toward the thing until my entire face came into overblown focus.

I have never been so horrified in my life. There were black rogue eyebrow hairs growing an inch outside of where any respectable brow hair should otherwise be, and the pores on my nose looked like dirty, cavernous sinkholes. There were eraser-size patches of dry, scaly skin everywhere and a subway map of tiny red veins around my nose. *I had a fucking moustache*—one that any fifteen-year-old boy would envy. How had I never noticed any of this before? I grabbed my youngest daughter, who was shopping with me, and thrust her perfect, dewy face in front of the glass. Magnified a dozen times it looked even more dewy and perfect, if that was at all possible. I suspect deep down I was hoping to find that the evil mirror had a handy knack for finding and highlighting flaws, but I realized in that moment that it simply made who-ever peered into it more of what she already was. Which in my case was a middle-aged woman in serious need of attention.

Naturally, I bought it. I love/hate that thing. I spend far too much time staring into it, and it makes me pick at things I shouldn't, but when I pluck my brows and do my makeup with that mirror and then turn the light off and flip the mirror to the unmagnified side, I'm usually pleasantly surprised by the results—compared to how I looked in floodlit, big-screen size, in any case. So at least there's that.

Unfortunately, now that leaving the house barefaced no longer feels like a viable option, I get to enjoy this experience a lot. I say *unfortunately* because I do not really like makeup. I can tolerate putting it on, but I hate taking it off, and with the exception of a brief blue eye shadow phase in the '80s, I've never been much into experimenting with it. Plus I really prefer the natural look. Dolly Parton famously said, "It takes a lot of money to look this cheap." I'd like to add that it takes an arsenal of makeup to look un-made-up if you're over forty and also want to appear halfway presentable.

Becuse the rules change as we get older, like it or not. Do a quick Internet search for "makeup to look younger" if you don't believe me. See those 178 million results? *Exactly.* You don't want to actually click on any of the links, of course, because your head might explode when you see all of the "here's how not to look like an old bat" articles alongside pictures of fourteen-year-old models.

To spare you that indignity, I'll distill the drill for you here: First, you need a makeup primer. Without it, your foundation will slide right off of your no-longer-supple skin and into a puddle on the floor, leaving you naked faced and sobbing, which is only a good look for Kristen Bell when her boyfriend surprises her by bringing home a sloth.* Speaking of founda-

---

* If you haven't seen this clip on *Ellen*, go find it on YouTube this instant. It's epic. Even funnier is the Auto-Tune version.

tion, yes, you need it, and yours better have light-reflecting particles in it, because youthful skin naturally reflects light (think Keira Knightley), while old skin sucks it up like a thirsty ShamWow (think Glenn Close as Cruella de Vil or the old guy with the pitchfork in Grant Wood's iconic *American Gothic*). Next, step away from the powder. I know you're all gung ho about that mineral crap because you saw it on QVC and it's supposed to be good for your skin and it has sunscreen right in it and you bought the fancy goat-hair brush to apply it with and everything—but after a certain point, powder is not your friend. Whereas a nice dusting of the stuff used to be a fine way to "set" your makeup, now it's a no-no because a matte finish highlights wrinkles—as does powder blush—so you're better off switching to a cream formula. (Which apparently you must apply *with your fingers* and above your cheekbones, not on or heaven forbid below them, so as not to draw attention to your sunken cheeks.) Give your babysitter or teenage niece your black eyeliner, and replace it with a softer brown model— the pros say its "much less jarring"—and never, ever put any shade of liner along your lower lashes, unless for some reason you're trying to accentuate the titanic dark circles you've got under there. Oh, and that lip liner you love? Use it, and you might as well tack a strip of marquee lights under your nose to highlight your craggy kisser. Add some pale, plumping gloss to your lips—never anything dark or flat—and a few fake eyelashes (yours aren't half what they used to be, sister), and you're as close to ready to face the world as you're going to get.

I mock this advice, but I also have to admit that I've tried it all. I bought a twenty-dollar egg-shaped makeup sponge because some famous makeup artist called it the "fountain of youth" in a magazine article. (It's a sponge. Shaped like an egg.) I've stopped using powder, and I switched to lighter lips and bought a brown liner. I prime the shit out of my skin before doing all of this, and sometimes, if I'm going out somewhere really special, I wear fake eyelashes. (When you buy them somewhere like MAC or Sephora instead of the drugstore, they'll put them on for you for *free*, which will save you a lot of cursing and also is a hell of a lot easier than curling your own anemic lashes and attempting to apply mascara, trust me.)

I was visiting my sixty-nine-year-old aunt Linda recently when I discovered the hands-down surefire way to being young and beautiful forever: Be Italian. Seriously, those damned Italians don't age. Unfortunately, I'm sort of screwed here. Although both of my parents sported plenty of Pisano blood, their English-Irish genes clearly dominated in all of their kids. Which means we share the same relatively fair skin that's prone to both sunburns and wrinkles. In other words, none of us is getting carded to buy booze anymore. Don't get me wrong; we don't quite resemble raisins yet. We just don't look all that much younger than our full-blooded Italian aunt with her still-gorgeous olive complexion. So, if there's any way you can be Italian when midlife hits, I highly recommend it.

"My Welcome-to-Midlife Moment Was . . ."

When I found a long gray hair growing out of my chin that appeared overnight.

—CLAIRE

There's an old Charles Schwab commercial I love where a clearly jaded sales manager is telling his team to go out and sell some patently crappy stocks. After he mentions the court-side playoff tickets for the rep who manages to unload the most, he ends his pep talk with, "Let's put some lipstick on this pig." It's a great visual and now something I think about a lot, especially when I happen to be putting on lipstick. I'll study myself in the mirror afterward and think, *Is this better now? Or was it better before? I think it was better before.* In fact, after employing a dozen or more methodical application methods based on the aforementioned anti-aging makeup commandments, more often than not I'm positive this pig looked better without any lipstick at all.

The key seems to be to start with a better-looking pig. (And please know that I am not calling anyone but myself a pig in what's become an admittedly fucked-up analogy here.) Barring plastic surgery—which I am not currently considering for a host of financial, emotional, practical, and irrational reasons I will detail later that include but are not limited to death and winding up looking like Carrot Top—I'm left with two alter-natives: convince the rest of the planet to stop going under the knife so we can be wrinkly and splotchy and patently past our primes together (and let's just face it right now that that's never going to happen), or figure out what I can do now—on the sly, for very little money, and with no risk of death or my husband finding out—to look as young and perky as I possibly can. Fine, there's a third option: I could just say screw it and stop wearing makeup or even making an effort, but I'm way too shallow for that, so we're back to the two.

Since it's cheap and I've never heard of anyone exfoliating themselves to death, I've started scrubbing my skin daily ever since the president of the American Academy of Dermatology said to me in a magazine interview, "I can tell the minute a patient walks into my office whether or not she exfoliates. The ones who do typically look ten years younger than their age." *Ten years*, you guys. That's your face-lift right there! So now I dutifully scour my face until it is bright red every single night. Sometimes my extra-super-gentle moisturizer stings when I put it on afterward, so I am pretty sure this means I'm doing a great job.

I've also tried to stop being sucked in by shiny magazine ads for fancy face creams with headlines like "Proven to Reduce Wrinkles up to 89%," because like you I am smart, and I recognize that the "up to" in there means "anything less than," which includes zero. Plus we all know that any product you can buy over-the-counter doesn't do squat, because if it did, we would all look like Megan Fox. Think about it. So no more crap. I wash with $10-a-gallon Cetaphil and a rough washcloth, moisturize with coconut oil, and squirrel away the money I'm not spending on overpriced promises for the day they open that drive-through, painless, incision-free, super-affordable, no-downtime face-lift center.

(What the hell do you *mean* nobody is working on that yet? If you're a scientist, would you kindly gather your smarty-pants friends together and get on that? The clock is ticking over here. The Mars rover can wait.)

A while ago I read that although side sleeping generally is recommended for postural alignment purposes, sleeping on your *back* is the secret if you want smoother skin.* In fact, the American Academy of Dermatology insists that people like me who enjoy lying belly down and smushing their faces into a pillow night after night will pay for it with permanent, lasting lines. (They liken the effects to what a shirt that's been folded in the bottom of your dresser drawer for weeks or years looks like when you pull it out. Even after you wear it for several hours, if you don't iron it, those folds never really smooth out.) But I'm a stomach sleeper, always have been. I try to assume the preferred pose; really, I do. And I usually can handle about thirty seconds of staring at the ceiling before I have to flip to my favored facedown position. Supposedly silk or satin pillowcases can help because they allow skin to slip right over the surface rather being forced into folds, but who wants to be sliding all over their bed all night? Plus I love my Egyptian cotton pillowcases, and also that shiny, silky shit is just a little too Hugh Hefner for me.

---

* Crippling spinal pain or a youthful visage? *Well, duh.*

If you're like me and refuse to drape your bed in porno film fabric, there's an exhaustive menu of "minimally invasive" remedies that promise to help mitigate these pesky signs of aging. They've got lasers and peels and pulsed lights and sonic lifts and cell freezing and radiofrequency therapies and a battery of injectables you can squeeze into just about any groove or contour you've got. Most of these things can be done on your lunch hour, and you can go right back to work, and the biggest risk is that somebody might think you snuck in a quick power nap because you look so goddamned refreshed.

I've spent hours online marveling at the before-and-after photos promoting every nonsurgical anti-aging treatment there is, but the problem I have with them is twofold: The first issue I have is that they're all temporary. I've endured the sensation of burning rubber bands smacking my face and lived for ten days looking like a leper to rid myself of some unattractive sun damage. I danced on my coffee table when the dark spots finally fell off and left a swath of pristine, unmarred skin in their wake. Then I wept hot, angry tears when those damned spots made a triumphant return just a few months later. I've injected a potentially deadly neurotoxin into my facial muscles and enjoyed seeing the skin above my brows turn as smooth as a river at dawn for three whole months before my face resumed its former ability to express emotion.* I still do it on occasion,

---

* You know, Botox, which Wikipedia describes as "the most acutely toxic substance known," but obviously, it's not *that* bad because it's FDA approved, and besides, everyone does it.

but to have a year-round line-free forehead would cost more than a grand a year (and possibly my marriage; see below), so if you see me sporting particularly thick bangs, you'll know why.

The second problem I have with these treatments is my husband. See, he is 110 percent against all of them. He thinks I'm "beautiful the way I am," a statement I am inclined to believe because I'm the one who buys his reading glasses in ever-increasing strengths, so I am almost positive he can barely even see me anymore. And while I know he's not the boss of me and I bring in my fair share of our family's income, I long ago gladly turned over our collective financial management to him, which means he gets to put the kibosh on spending he deems unnecessary. He swears he's anti-anti-aging simply because I don't need it, but I know it's because he's super-conservative and thinks it's far more important to pay our mortgage and put aside a few bucks for the kids' college educations and to set it up so that we might not have to work until the day we drop dead at our desks than to have a hotter, younger-looking wife. So I've acquiesced. I've also made it patently clear that if we find ourselves on the receiving end of a financial windfall, he's taking the kids to Disney Land on his own, because I'm checking into the nearest medispa for at least three weeks.

Until that day, I will keep doing what I'm doing, which is mostly exfoliating and waiting.

CHAPTER 2

I Feel Bad about My Knees

After the getting-closer-to-death bit and having to learn all new makeup rules, the third worst part about aging is watching your body fall apart before your very eyes. (I figured we'd get the vanity crap over with early in this book, and then we can get to other fun stuff like figuring out how we're going to pay for our funerals and the ~~likelihood~~ remote possibility that we all drink too much.) It seems like every single day I notice something—a bump, a mole, an extra chin, a three-inch hair growing out of my ear—that I am almost positive wasn't there yesterday. Then I feel bad because I didn't think to appreciate the thing's *not* being there when I was lucky enough not to be saddled with it.

Seriously, I know we're all enlightened these days and we're supposed to love and embrace our imperfections, which I would be happy to do if it weren't totally impossible. Did you read Nora Ephron's swan song, *I Feel Bad about My Neck*? I did, as soon as it hit the shelves. With all due respect to the memory of the funniest woman ever to write a fake orgasm scene, when I read that title, I looked at my own reflection and thought, *Really? Just your neck?* What about your flabby arms? Your saggy, shapeless ass? Your spider veiny ankles? Your midsection that resembles a deflated balloon lying atop a pile of dead snakes? Your mushy, squishy muffin top? That area that you used to refer to as your décolletage that now looks like some sort of seagoing traffic map, with a cluster of creeks all flowing southward into one big river that dams up between your south-facing post-baby boobs? The back fat that spills over your bra strap, even if you're at your lifetime-lowest weight? Good Lord, your feet?* (I don't know about yours, but mine are a mess. Bunions, bone spurs, fallen arches, plantar fasciitis, tendonitis, cracked heels, hammer toes—you name it, I've got it. My feet might be the reason those particular body parts are referred to as "dogs." In fact, my awesome and loving but also brutally honest uncle Jack insists I should not be allowed to wear flip-flops in public.) And that was eight years ago. If I had to pick a single body part to bemoan and then write a book about it today, we'd be here a long time.

Just for fun, let's start with cellulite. According to experts,†

---

* To be clear, I'm talking about *my* decrepit body parts here, not Nora's.

† You know when I say that, I mean a quick Google search, right?

upward of 95 percent of women have it, and I am one of them. (Except, inexplicably, when I am naked in the fitting room at Anthropologie. I don't know if it's the lighting or the slight tilt they give to the mirrors, or maybe they're pumping extra oxygen under the doors and I'm unwittingly stoned whenever I am in there, but honest to God I look like an airbrushed teenager in those fitting rooms. For obvious reasons, I am in there a lot.) I had a chance to get rid of my cottage cheese, too—not only would it have been free, but I actually would have gotten paid—but I turned it down.

Allow me to explain. As a freelance writer, I have written hundreds of beauty articles for women's magazines over the years. When you do this for a living, cosmetics companies ship you truckloads of stuff to sample and review. Then if you write about it, the magazine pays you for your "research" and writing. The products are a nice perk, no doubt. If I lined up all of my free eyeliners end to end, they'd stretch from my house to the nearest Target (which, for the record, is thirty long miles away). Anyway, for a story on cellulite I was sent several thousand dollars worth of fancy skin-smoothing creams. I am not exaggerating. For weeks my office was a maze of boxes brimming with lotions and potions specially developed for every imperfect body part I own. One company even gifted me my very own endermologie machine—a $2,000 vacuum-like gizmo with a wand you simply "rubbed over any trouble spots" (as if there were but one or two!) a few times a week. Can you imagine? Smooth, dimple-free skin was within my grasp for the first time in my adult life. I couldn't wait to get started.

I religiously vacuumed myself and applied these very expensive but free-to-me creams to my body, ready to watch those nasty dimples disappear. By "religiously" I mean I did this every single day. For *three whole days*.

Then I just sort of gave up.

Let me reiterate right here that I have cellulite. It's not life threatening or anything, but I hate it and I wish I didn't have it, and because of it I'm one of those gals who tucks her towel around her lower half to walk four feet from her lounge chair to the pool's edge. But I made little more than a half-assed attempt to fix it, even when a purported fix literally was dropped into my lap. Was it because I secretly didn't mind my lumpy, bumpy body? I can confidently and emphatically say no. Was the expected effort too great? I'll remind you that all I had to do was vacuum myself and then rub a little pleasantly scented lotion onto my various pock-marked body parts on a quasi-regular basis. Was it because I secretly didn't think these magic bullets would work? Maybe. But I had them and other people bought them and they cost a flipping fortune and surely they couldn't hurt, so you'd think I'd at least give it a wholehearted whirl.

But I didn't. I'd like to think that it's because I have reached a wise, mature, and enlightened point in my life where I realize that I am more than the mere sum or state of my body parts. I've faced the realities of aging and embraced the truth that my body is here to transport me from one enjoyable activity to the next, not to serve as some specimen of impossible perfection or a hunk of meat to be alternately ogled or envied. I've learned to respect my physical form for what it does—houses and protects my vital organs, provides a handy hat rest, and makes impossibly beautiful babies—and not what it looks like. I've gazed at my naked self in the mirror and smiled at the woefully, wonderfully imperfect shape staring back at me, this vessel I was given to carry my soul and my memories from cradle to grave, and thanked my body for being such a kind and intrepid steward.

You didn't actually buy a word of that, did you?

I said I'd *like* to think that's why I didn't use those stupid products. But since that's a bunch of bullshit, I'll tell you the truth: I was too damned lazy. Yes, I couldn't be bothered to apply a combination of sucking and smearing in exchange for a twenty-year-old's ass.

I know. I make me sick, too.

In my defense, I've never been the layaway type. When I want something, I want it now. I am the reason—well, not personally but people *like* me—that cosmetic surgery is an eleventy-trillion-dollar-a-year industry in the United States Sure, we could run to Hawaii and back (metaphorically, obviously) to lose our belly blubber. Or we could just ask a nice surgeon to make a discreet abdominal incision, jam his barbaric but effective cannula through it, and suck out that bothersome fat. That way we can be skinny by next Friday, which frankly seems an awfully long time away, but we suppose we can endure the wait.

If we are so inclined (and can find ten to eighty grand lying around, which, believe me, I have tried without success), we can fix our every last flaw, and relatively quickly. We can have our floppy tummies tucked, our thinning hair transplanted, our wispy lips and sinking eye sockets and hollow cheeks plumped with fillers (so round and youthful!). If our breasts and butts are as high and firm as ripe, hanging fruit, we can lay down for smoother, rounder, plumper earlobes. (I shit you not.) We can have our *knees lifted*, for fuck's sake, another procedure I heard about (thanks Demi Moore!) that left me staring southward with the sad realization that I probably wasn't looking hard enough to find body parts to loathe.

And while I don't even hate to admit that I would do it all if I bled time and money—all of it!*—did you ever stop to think about how totally and irrefutably *insane* the whole thing is? Of course you didn't, because everybody does it, and for the most part they look really good, too. (Except Donatella Versace, La Toya Jackson, Priscilla Presley, Melanie Griffith, Joan Van Ark, Janice Dickinson, and Mickey Rourke, all of whom can be immediately negated with a single full-body shot of fifty-one-year-old Demi.) But imagine for a moment that there's an undiscovered civilization out there on the former-planet Pluto, and young Plutonians are studying modern-day Earthlings in all of their narcissistic glory.

---

* Well, if I were guaranteed not to die and to get a fabulous, natural result. And probably never a full face-lift because I saw a really disturbing *Dateline* on it, and try as I might, I can never unsee those images of unconscious women with pen marks all over their faces lying there looking dead while a doctor sliced right through their skin and tissues and muscles like a Harvard-trained Hannibal Lecter.

"Ewwwwww, no freaking way," screams Elborg. Elborg is a thirteen-year-old Plutonian sitting in her Universal Studies class, twirling her antennae and learning about faraway customs, like Easter and Hanukkah and face-lifts. "They cut the front of their heads open, snip away the extra skin, pull the rest of it really tight, and then sew it back together! And they think this makes them more attractive! Even though their faces all look the same and don't match the rest of their bodies so they have to wear turtlenecks for the rest of ever! And get this: Sometimes humans die from the sleeping medicine, and they know this is a possibility, but they do it anyway! Wow, Earthlings are *wacked*. But a giant bunny who brings you chocolate and eight days of presents would be pretty cool."

I don't want anyone to cut my face open, ever. First of all, what if I died on the table, then everyone would know that I was vain and selfish, and I wouldn't even be alive to defend myself. (And by "defend myself" I mean "blame everyone I know who did it before me and made me feel old and ugly in comparison.") Plus—and this part can bring me to tears, and I'm not even considering going under the knife—I'm a *mom*. I have young, innocent daughters who love me and think I'm beautiful and depend on me to drive them to volleyball and explain things like how tampons work that their father can't or at least probably shouldn't. I want them to love themselves at their age and mine, pimples and droopy knees and all. I want to meet their future husbands and hold their unborn babies and guilt them into picking me over their someday in-laws to spend holidays with, and it would be a shame to miss out on all of that just because my stomach skin looks like I stole it from a Shar-Pei and I'm getting a little jowly.

As a media professional, I hate it that people are always blaming the body-dissatisfaction epidemic on the unrealistic images presented in magazines and movies. Listen, it's not the *media's* fault. The media is just the delivery system. Blaming them (us) would be like blaming the hot dog if the ketchup was bad. The problem is obviously Hollywood, where people clearly have way more money than sense, and already gorgeous gals do shit like *undergo ten plastic surgery procedures in a single day* and apparently nearly die but still blab to *People* magazine that it was "totally worth it."

Yes, Heidi Montag, I'm talking about you.

To quote every person on Twitter all day every day, WTF? In the *People* piece, Montag asks, "Who is anyone to judge me?" (She also goes on to confess that she "was an ugly duckling before" and adds that she's "really excited for the world to see the new me, the real me," two comments that make me want to punch her in the surgically perfect nose.) To answer her rather glib question: I judge you, honey. And I have every right to, because you—with your implant-enhanced peach of an ass and your tiny liposucked waist and your complete lack of nasolabial folds and your ridiculously perky boobs the size of my head—are raising the bar so impossibly high, at the tender age of twenty-seven, that the rest of us pretty much want to throw in the towel.

In case you aren't convinced that Ms. Montag is single-handedly to blame for your derriere dissatisfaction, consider her response to the reporter's "are you finished with plastic surgery" question: "I'm just starting," the impossibly blonde bombshell insisted. "As you get older, there are so many different treatments—all the big celebrities get their spider veins removed. Let's just say there's a lot of maintenance. Nobody ages perfectly, so I plan to keep using surgery to make me as perfect as I can be. Because, for me, the surgery is always so rewarding."

Surgery is so *rewarding*? No, dear, making sandwiches and delivering them to a homeless shelter is rewarding. Teaching your child to ride a bike is rewarding. Earning a diploma, learning Italian, baking homemade bread, delivering a meaningful eulogy, growing heirloom tomatoes, writing an old-fashioned letter to your grandmother in gigantic block print, holding a ninety-second plank, popping a perfectly ripe zit without drawing blood: all rewarding. Granted, spending tens of thousands of dollars to look like a human Barbie doll might make you batshit giddy when you look in the mirror, but I'd hesitate to call it rewarding.

Let me reiterate: I'm not necessarily against a little subtle cosmetic enhancement. (If you are and think less of me because I'm not, kindly refer to the disclaimer at the beginning of this book.) And to be fair, I don't know a single gal who's walking around in a wholly natural state. We're all doing whatever we can to mask, mitigate, or at least deflect attention from what's happening to what nature gave us. We dye and straighten and style our frizzy old-lady hair, whiten our teeth, and smear extra-thick, spackle-like foundation all over our faces. We wear tights to hide our spider veins and cellulite and age spots, and pretend to love turtlenecks so we can conceal our sagging necks. We struggle into Spanx (more on that later) and sport bras that have more padding than a bed pillow to create the illusion that our bodies aren't morphing into mush. As one friend put it, "Some people wear their fake boobs in their bras; others wear them underneath their skin . . . what's the difference?" You have to admit she has a point. I just wish the surgical option didn't exist in the first place so I didn't have to be simultaneously horrified and enticed by it, or feel like I'm supposed to measure up to the gals who've had bumper-to-bumper work done.

It's actually not at all fair when you think about it. In our grandmother's generation, if you looked great at a certain age, it was because you'd taken good care of yourself.* You'd *earned* it. You'd shunned the sun and done your calisthenics and passed up every delectable dessert you were ever offered, and you had youthful skin and an enviable waistline and the ideal 1:1 face-to-chin ratio because of it. But now, anybody who's willing and financially able to succumb to the scalpel can look younger and better than you do, and all of the sun shunning and jumping jacks and salad eating in the world won't tip the scales in your favor.

Of course, there are alternatives to surgery. Like working out (awful) and dieting (worse) and self-tanner (stinky but

---

* Or you were born Italian, in which case you just got lucky.

definitely less awful). Self-tanner might be my favorite invention of this century. If you're not convinced that everyone looks fifteen pounds thinner and fifteen years younger with a fake tan, check out the before-and-after pictures in any weight-loss product advertisement. Before: lumpy, bumpy, and pasty-ass white; after: taut, toned, and the color of melted caramel. Coincidence? I think not.

If you're a self-tanning virgin, there are several things you should know. First of all, you can pay eight dollars for a bottle of the drugstore cream, thirty dollars for a fancy department store brand, or fifty dollars for a salon experience. I'm not here to tell you how to spend your money, but it's worth noting that they all use the same ingredient to stain your skin, and they all get all over everything you wear and make you smell like a rotting pelican carcass until you can shower (generally four to eight hours after application). But *fifteen pounds and fifteen years*! No stain, no gain.

I never felt any need to cheat on my eight-dollar drugstore tanning cream until I accidentally purchased a certificate for a professional tropical spray tan at my kids' school auction. I didn't really consider the fact at the time that by "professional" it meant *somebody else would be putting it on my body.* (It was a fund-raiser, okay? And also I may have been drunk. But if I was, I was drunk shopping for *my children*, or their art and PE classes or iPads for the classrooms or new solar panels or something, so try not to judge.) Anyway, that certificate sat in my desk for eleven months, because every time I went to book my professional tropical spray tan, I was reminded that I generally try to avoid getting naked in front of a complete stranger, "professional" or not. That's when I would decide that I was Far Too Busy that week and put it off. Again.

Then my friend Barb called.

"Want to go with me to get a spray tan before spring break?" she asked. Barb was heading off on a cruise and I was going to Florida, and obviously, we'd both be baring a lot of (old, white, flabby) skin. I was about to decline—who had the time or money for such luxuries?—when I remembered the certificate.

"I'm in," I told her, praying that the spray-tan lady was older, whiter, or flabbier than me—preferably all three.

Of course, she was adorable. And also younger, tanner, and much, much fitter.

"You can just undress in there and come back out when you're ready," Britney informed me, pointing toward a bathroom. (Her name wasn't really Britney. But it may as well have been.)

And walk from there to here buck-ass naked while you're just standing there watching, you perverted freak?

"Oh, do you want some paper panties?" Brit asked as I shuffled toward the bathroom.

"I think I'm good," I muttered, closing the door behind me.

I'd worn my tiniest thong underwear—the kind that's basically a string up your butt and around your hips with a small triangle of fabric in the front. Why I felt compelled to cover just this one ugly part when I'd be baring 3,458 other ugly parts is a bit of a mystery even to me, but it somehow felt more appropriate. Wearing only this scrap of elastic and Lycra, a paper shower cap, and a smirk—a super attractive look, I might add—I trudged out of the bathroom and over to the tanning booth.

"Okay, stand right in the middle, then spread your legs nice and wide, and raise your arms out to your sides," Brit instructed me, scrutinizing the job in front of her through scrunched up eyes. "Can you lift your boobs up any higher? No? Well, maybe bend forward a little. Maybe a little more. Oh, never mind."

I rotated naked in front of her for six years, trying to tighten my abs and flex my triceps and retain my dignity, which I quickly found out is totally impossible to do simultaneously. As humiliating as the whole experience was, when Britney was done airbrushing parts of my body my gynecologist has never seen and I looked in the mirror, I swooned at the sight of my younger, leaner-looking self. I drove home ridiculously pleased with myself.

Then I undressed. *Huh, that's funny,* I thought as I checked out my rear view. *That little T-shaped bar where my thong was looks awfully high. In fact, it sort of looks like it's halfway up my back. But that can't be. Because if it were, you'd see it when I put on my bikini bottoms.* Certainly Britney would have noticed this, being a professional and everything.

So I put on my bikini bottoms to check. They sat a good two inches below the T-shaped bar, which poked out above my bottoms and sort of looked like one of those steer skulls you see in a lot of Southwestern décor. My friend Hannah said I should bedazzle it (because of course I took a picture and sent it to everyone I know and then posted it on my blog); other friends said maybe people would think it was a birthmark or a tattoo. At the end of the day, I decided that nobody was looking at my ass anyway—at least I certainly hoped they weren't, tramp stamp or not—and I bravely went on my trip and did my best to rock my white stripe. But do let my stupidity be a lesson to you.

If that little story puts you off fake tanner forever, maybe the answer for you is Skinnies. You know about these, right? I saw them first in a discount department store, but apparently they debuted on *Shark Tank*, the show where aspiring entrepreneurs pitch their million-dollar ideas to investors in the hopes that one of them will pony up the cash to help launch their businesses. In this case the idea was Skinnies Instant Lifts, a handy, nonsurgical option for masking extra flab on your arms, thighs, tummy, muffin top, and hips. I'm sure the Skinnies people have a whole spiel about their high-tech product design, but I'll just summarize it for you: It's basically tape. You see, you just stick one end of the clear adhesive strip to the lowest part of your sagging skin and then yank on the tape, affixing the other end up nice and high. The result is a perfectly smooth tape-covered tangle of extra flesh and skin. "Hides under shorts, skirts, and tops," a video promoting the products insists. "Nobody will know but you!" (And maybe the friend you have to enlist to help you pull those giant strips off because I'm guessing that shit takes balls.) The sharks passed on the inventors' equity offer, but apparently there's a market for Skinnies—the show's website claims they sold seventy-five-thousand-bucks' worth of skin tape in the first five months. They even make a waterproof version the maker claims "you can wear under your skirted swimsuit," as if the mere fact that you're sporting a skirted swimsuit isn't depressing enough without having to worry about someone catching a glimpse of your taped-up ass underneath it.

I think I'll pass. But I like knowing Skinnies are out there, because now when I see some impossibly fit-looking woman my age, I can totally assume that the reason she looks so great is because she's wearing several yards of tape beneath her Lululemon yoga pants.

CHAPTER 3

Hair Is a Full-Time Job

Now that we've all agreed to try our best to become Italian and stop filling plastic surgeons' pockets with cash we don't technically have, I suppose we should talk about hair. Jesus. After a certain point, keeping that shit looking presentable is a constant, exhausting, losing battle, like holding on to an umbrella in a tornado . . . uphill in the snow, wearing banana slippers, and carrying an angry, pregnant porcupine.

Now, before you get all "Embrace your gray! It's elegant and chic and sophisticated" on me, allow me to point out that when my hair turned more salt than pepper, it also assumed the texture of a Hungarian Wirehaired Vizsla and decided to completely defy gravity and grow *out* instead of down. Remember Rosanne Rosannadanna from *Saturday Night Live*? That. But less attractive.

In high school, I had a French teacher who washed her waist-length hair exactly once a week. You could tell this because she had a hairstyle schedule that revolved around that weekly event. The first clean-mane day she wore it long and loose, parted hippie style right down the middle. On day two, she pulled the sides up into matching barrettes. Day three she'd add a braid to each side of her face and gather them in the back; on days four and five the braids, along with the rest of the length, would get bound into a ponytail. On day six—if you were lucky enough to run into her at a football game or school play—you'd see she had inexplicably wrapped the side braids up and over her head (which was by now beginning to resemble a freshly greased skillet). Day seven was usually some clusterfuck of shiny, slimy braids all tangled Medusa fashion about her skull. Mercifully, this look meant that it was almost time to lather up again.

My current hair-coloring schedule, sadly, looks a lot like that but is drawn out into a three-week pattern and simplified a bit and minus the braids. Week one, after my roots are freshly dyed, I can wear my hair any old way I please—pulled back into a ponytail, swept into a messy bun, blown out or straightened or curled, bangs or no bangs. This week goes by very quickly. Week two, a nice white stripe appears *out of fucking nowhere* down my part, and my temples start to look ashy, so there's no more pulling it back. I apply some color—at home, by myself—to these spots, just to get through the next ten days, and pray that there's no wind in the forecast. Week three

I mostly wear hats and stay home a lot, trying to avoid any social interaction until I can make it to my next salon appointment. This week feels like it lasts seventeen months.

When I was young, I cursed my baby-fine, stick-straight, couldn't-hold-a-curl hair. I wanted to be Farrah Fawcett, damn it, but I was lucky to be Kate Jackson on the best of all hair days. No matter how much time I spent primping and curling and teasing that mess or how much White Rain I shellacked it with afterward, it looked like a frozen lake at sunrise within fifteen minutes. It was smooth and glassy when I wanted big and fluffy, and I honestly couldn't imagine pulling a worse card in the hair lottery. Hahahahaha, I tell the stupid young bitch that I was. She clearly had no idea.

What I would give for wake-and-go hair again. Oh, I still can have a halfway decent looking 'do; it just requires several hours and an entire cabinet full of products to achieve and maintain it. Without that effort, I scare children—and I mean that literally. Just recently, while I was fixing my morning cup of coffee and hadn't braved a glance in the mirror yet, my oldest daughter came into the kitchen. Her slippers made skid marks on the tile when she saw me.

"Mom, what happened to your *hair*?" she asked, appalled.

"I don't know," I replied, absentmindedly patting it with my hands. I'd gone to bed with wet hair the night before, which is never a wise move on my part. "What's wrong with it?"

"It looks like a rat got into it and built a nest," she informed me. I ventured a peek in the hall mirror. She'd sort of nailed it with that description.

According to my hairdresser, the answer is some kind of fancy chemical blowout that originated in Brazil. Because those fucking Brazilians haven't tortured me enough with their god-awful butt-crack waxes and itty-bitty bikinis. Now I'm supposed to wrap my head in formaldehyde, a known carcinogen, and walk around looking like a Vaseline-coated rat (no clips, ponytails, or hats allowed!) for several days while the deadly toxins fully penetrate my hair to remove the frizz—for five minutes or until the regrowth appears. Never mind that the treatment costs several hundred dollars a pop, has been banned in Canada and Europe, and has potential side effects including blurred vision, headaches, dizziness, wheezing, throat irritation, nausea, nose bleeds, chest pain, and rashes. We're talking about Gisele Bündchen hair! Unless, of course, you die from the fumes or it all falls out, which apparently can happen if you believe everything you read online. Clearly, buttery-smooth supermodel locks come with a price. Call me a penny-pinching chickenshit, but it's not one I'm prepared to pay.

This does not mean I am willing to live with frizz. I use glossing shampoos and smoothing balms and straightening sprays, and do weekly conditioning treatments. When I style my hair—which I will admit isn't often because I work at home and I am almost certain my mail carrier, who is the only other adult I see most days, doesn't give a rat's ass what my hair looks like—it's an event involving clips and sections and a huge round tourmaline ceramic brush and another flat-paddle model. I aim the blow-dryer *down* the hair shaft like you're supposed to and don't stop until every last strand is bone dry, even when my arms are quivering from the effort. (Confession: I even invested in a $200 ionic blow-dryer because it was supposed to give me flatter hair. I know a lot of you swear by your negatively charged blowguns—my sister once left hers in a hotel room and made her husband drive six roundtrip hours to retrieve it—but all mine gave me was a flatter wallet.) After a coating of anti-frizz shine spray I whip out the hair mascara, which is exactly what it sounds like and sort of helps tame the halo of flyaway hairs that sticks up in every direction and makes me look like one of those troll pencil toppers no matter how diligent I am about styling. Then, as often as not, I look in the mirror, decide it still looks like crap, and throw on a hat.

It's exhausting, all of it.

Maybe the problem is that my hair is still long. It almost always has been. I've tried cutting it a few times over the years, but I always regret it within two days. The last time I chopped off a significant bit of it—into a stylish, blunt, chin-length bob exactly like Jennifer Aniston was sporting at the time—I was in my mid-thirties and had just had my first baby. "You got the mom cut!" my (much) younger brother said when he saw it. "Are you going to get a minivan now, too?"

"Jennifer Aniston has this haircut, and she's not a mom," I informed him with as much self-control as I could muster. "It's chic."

"If you say so," he replied with a shrug.

I immediately went out and pierced my nose. I am not lying. I pushed my newborn baby into a tattoo parlor in her stroller to have it done, too. I was *that* determined to prove to the world (or at least my brother) that I hadn't gone to the land of control-top jeans and sensible shoes yet. Right away I loved my little cubic zirconia stud and felt young and hip again just for having it, but the back of the post always poked out of my nostril and made me feel like there was a big booger dangling there. I was constantly having to tuck it back in, which made me worry people would think I was a dust junkie trying to wipe away a trail of cocaine, which would be particularly in-excusable what with my new baby and all. Plus makeup would get caked around the stud, and sometimes it itched, and all in all it turned out to be a big, fat pain in the nose. When my hair grew to an acceptable, non-mom-cut length again (to clarify: my head hair, not my nose hair), I took out my fake-diamond stud and let the hole close up.

I'm not sure what the cutoff is on long hair, either. It seems like most women gradually go shorter and shorter as they get older, and while I don't want to be one of those ladies with a long, nasty gray braid down her back, I'm not really into the Jamie Lee Curtis look, either. You really have to have a great face to pull off the pixie crop, and I'm not saying I'm ugly or anything, but if you've seen me in a hair-towel turban I'm sure you'd agree that when it comes to hair, the more I have the better I look.

One of my best friends is my age and still has Pantene commercial hair. It's six miles long and a gorgeous shade of red and as thick as a horse's tail and truly nauseating in its lusciousness. People stop her on the street to tell her how spectacular her hair is—*as if she doesn't know.* I mean, it's not like she's got a bit of lettuce in her teeth or she sat in bird shit and can't see it. She lives with this hair, all day every day! (Just once I want her to reply, "Wow, really? I have fabulous hair? Thanks for letting me know!" But I guess that could come off as bitchy.) I've known this woman since we were fourteen years old, and I envied her magnificent mane back then, but now I'd stand buck naked on a busy street corner at rush hour for the chance to rock those locks for even a single day. Because fat, lustrous hair screams *I AM A YOUNG AND VIBRANT GODDESS*, something that will get you crazy stares or an arrest warrant if your mouth is the part doing the screaming.

"I can't even wear my hair up because it's so heavy I get a headache after five minutes," Pantene Girl tries to complain.

"Cry me a fucking river," I reply sympathetically.

"It takes an hour and a half to blow it dry," she pouts.

"You poor, unlucky soul," I say. "How ever do you manage?"

"I have to pay extra for my highlights," she protests.

"If you tell me your eyes burn from the constant, blinding reflection of your shiny, healthy hair in the mirror, I will sneak into your house and fill your conditioner bottle with Nair," I tell her sweetly.

If you're not convinced that hair continues to be a particularly big deal at any age, consider how much press FLOTUS Michelle Obama got last year after a simple haircut. (She got bangs! OMG!) Every major news network reported on it, along with outlets from the *Huffington Post* to the *Daily Beast* and *E! Online.* Naturally, the First Lady felt the need to respond to the raging hoopla. "This is my midlife crisis, the bangs," she told Rachael Ray. "I couldn't get a sports car. They won't let me bungee jump. So instead, I cut my bangs."

I have bangs already (on account of my "fivehead" and also the price of Botox), but I know how she feels. You just look in that mirror, and everything else is going south, and you want a change—something you can do quickly, this minute, before anyone can try to talk you out of it—to feel different, to look different, to *be* different. I've dabbled with peacock feathers and pink streaks, added more lowlights and brighter highlights and changed my base color. I've dyed the whole mess platinum and espresso and every shade in between. Finally I bought these human-hair clip-in extensions (I call them my Lee Press-On Hairs) that aren't super comfortable but turn my hair from dull and scrawny to dazzling and substantial faster than you can say *curl up and dye.*

My husband once saw a chunk of my fake hair lying on the bathroom counter. He'd seen the things *in* my hair, of course, but apparently when I'm wearing them, they are a lot less terrifying.

"What the hell is *that*?" he screamed, pointing to the tangle of strands with a horrified look on his face.

"It's my clip-in hair," I chirped, picking it up and stroking it lovingly.

"Jesus, I thought it was a dead gerbil," he said, shaking his head.

It actually really did look like a gerbil,* so now we call any fake hair a "gerbil." This is great fun, because we'll be at dinner, and he'll lean forward and whisper "there's a gerbil at four o'clock," and then I'll try to casually scope it out and see if he's right. He's getting really good at spotting them, too. At a wedding recently, sitting in the church—where I was too busy waiting for lightning to strike me dead just for being there to be checking out the 'dos—he leaned over and very seriously said, "I'm not positive, but I think I counted more than fifty gerbils in here." (I actually wanted to name this book *Fifty Gerbils in a Church*, but some people thought that was too obscure.) The point of this story is that I am not the only gerbil buyer or wearer out there, so clearly, I'm not the only one trying to recapture—or at least hang on to—the vestiges of my fleeting youth by whatever artificial means I can get my hands on.

Did I really just admit all of that?

---

* But I'd argue that it looked as much like a live gerbil as a dead one.

CHAPTER 4

Where Did All of This Shit Come From?

My maternal grandparents lived forever in a tiny, tidy house. Hoarders they were not. When my grandma died at ninety-three, I helped my mom go through her stuff and decide who would get what. I remember sliding open a dresser drawer and marveling at how light it was and how there was all of this room, this *air*, in that drawer. With a soft swish of your hand, you could easily see all three nightgowns and the two identical slips she owned. Her closet was the same: a smattering of hangers, each inches apart, that moved and swayed freely when you pulled open the doors. Everywhere we went in that house, closets and cabinets held only the barest of essentials.

To this day, I cannot fathom how she did it. My house is three times the size hers was, and we are bursting at the seams over here. My bedroom closet is a converted former bathroom—big enough so that I can stretch out on the floor and hide from my kids when I am on the phone*—and still there's so much shit crammed in there that I find things "hanging" that aren't even on hangers but merely being suspended by the helpful army of garments on either side. I have seven kitchen drawers—my grandma had one—each packed so tightly, so meticulously, that a homeless paperclip would be hard-pressed to find a sliver of real estate in any one of them.

We live in a different world than my grandmother did, though, namely one that has enticing infomercials and As Seen on TV stores where you can shop for all of the world's must-have inventions in one convenient place. Throw in modern conveniences like eBay and Groupon and free shipping on orders over $25, and multiply it by a few kids who collect acorns and sea glass and bottle tops and erasers, and compound it all with the reality that there's a gadget or gizmo to solve our every unknown problem and unrecognized need, and it's no wonder that here I am in my life's back nine,† gravely at risk of being overtaken by stuff.

The bottom line is that while our grandparents knew how to get by with mere necessities, we are a generation of consum-

---

* Hell YEAH, I do this. It takes them forever to find me, too.

† I am pretty sure that's a golf expression. I generally try to avoid sports references as I know nothing at all about any of them (except tennis, where I'm almost positive the goal is to get the ball *over* the net), but a friend used this recently, and I liked it, so I stole it.

ers. If they make it, we buy it.* We trade in our hard-earned cash for Slankets (They're blankets! With sleeves! What a concept!) and Rechargeable Heated Slippers and Wineglass Holder Necklaces—which incidentally are all things you can purchase right now, even if you are reading this book on an airplane, from the *SkyMall* catalog.

I hear a lot of talk from friends lately about *simplifying*. This is a big buzzword now, but as far as I can tell, it's just another way of saying "getting rid of crap you don't need," which I think we can all agree is really fucking hard. Because as you probably know, the world is filled with very tempting, often darling, and sometimes even useful things that we may not technically *need* but really rather enjoy.

Take the majority of your kitchen tools, for example. The jobs performed by your cheese slicer, vegetable peeler, apple corer, hot dog dicer, mini chopper, melon baller, garlic press, mezzaluna, mandoline, zester, grater, and poultry shears could all pretty much be performed by one decent knife. Yes, it would be painstaking to carve out tiny, uniform orbs of melon—but it could be done. Or you could have yourself some nice melon squares and call it a day.

If you're not fully convinced of our collective consumerism, I present to you the Hutzler 571 Banana Slicer. Yes, folks, there is a gadget that will assume that tricky task of hacking an unwieldy banana into identical, manageable pieces. The Amazon reviews—and there are currently 4,760 of them—are priceless.

---

* I don't know if *you* buy it, but I certainly do. It's sort of a sore subject in my house, so maybe don't bring it up if you come over for dinner.

Mrs. Toledo from Greeley, Ohio, gives the Hutzler 571 five stars, writing:

> *What can I say about the 571B Banana Slicer that hasn't already been said about the wheel, penicillin, or the iPhone . . . this is one of the greatest inventions of all time. My husband and I would argue constantly over who had to cut the day's banana slices. It's one of those chores NO ONE wants to do! You know, the old "I spent the entire day rearing OUR children, maybe YOU can pitch in a little and cut these bananas?" and of course, "You think I have the energy to slave over your damn bananas? I worked a 12 hour shift just to come home to THIS?!" These are the things that can destroy an entire relationship. It got to the point where our children could sense the tension. The minute I heard our 6-year-old girl in her bedroom, re-enacting our daily banana fight with her Barbie dolls, I knew we had to make a change. That's when I found the 571B Banana Slicer. Our marriage has never been healthier, AND we've even incorporated it into our lovemaking. THANKS 571B BANANA SLICER!*

I will have you know that I do not own a banana slicer. *Because obviously that is a ridiculous invention.* But I have all of those other kitchen gadgets I mentioned (plus an avocado slicer, which I am calling out in particular because it is a very different and necessary tool, and if you eat avocados with any regularity, it will change your life). I can't seem to help it. I buy stuff I like only marginally because it's on sale at a price that's too impossible for me to resist, a compulsion I inherited from my mom. If a three-dollar item is marked ten for ten bucks, I'll grab ten, even though I know that you get the $1/item price no matter how many you buy. I stockpile things that seem handy or revolutionary—like empty bottles with sponge tips you can fill with touch-up paint and long-handled brushes designed for the singular purpose of cleaning the lint trap in your dryer, and avocado slicers, which I believe has been established are both handy *and* revolutionary.

Compounding my little shopping compulsion that we're not going to talk about is the reality that I am not one of those heartless people who can stuff my children's macaroni neck-laces and ALL ABOUT ME posters immediately into the trash. I also have a hell of a time parting with the eleven-pound Restoration Hardware catalog they send every three months, because I feel personally responsible for the hectare of trees that sacrificed their lives to produce its glossy pages. I hang on to the stack of gossip magazines I bought for the plane because there's a Sticky Thai Cod in Peanut Sauce recipe I want in this one and an ad for some new lash-extending mascara in another one and an article about the *far-younger-than-me* new female Yahoo! CEO in yet another that I plan to send to my sister, and someday, when I have more time, I have every intention of cooking/buying/sending these things.*

Because I do not want to be one of those people you read

---

* We both know I will never, ever cook, buy, or send any of them.

about in the news who dies in a tragic house fire because the firefighters *can't get through all of my crap to save me*, my only choice is to be organized. I might have a shit-ton of stuff, but every single item is categorically sorted and stowed. My medicine closet has separate bins for adult and kid formulas, first aid paraphernalia, and personal grooming supplies. My daughters' toys are separated into individual, labeled boxes for dress-up clothes and accessories, baby dolls, Barbies, stuffed animals, board games, sports gear, Legos, electronics, musical instruments, and my personal favorite "Miscellaneous Hard Toys." (This is where we store Slinkys, marbles, plastic pirate money, key chains, fake phones, super-bouncy balls, and other not-plush toys that aren't copious enough to warrant their own bin. And yes, my kids refer to it as Miscellaneous Hard Toys, as in "Mom! Come look! There's a stuffed animal in Miscellaneous Hard Toys! Isn't that *silly*?") Since we have enough art supplies to open our own Michaels, the crafty crap is further sorted (stickers, cutting implements, paper, adhesive products, paint supplies, crayons, chalk, charcoal, etc.) in a plastic "art tower" with removable drawers. Our garage walls are lined with containers neatly packed with camping equipment, ski gear, beach supplies, electrical miscellany, pet necessities, and extraneous hardware. Even my sock drawer is subdivided by type (athletic, dress, ugly but soft and good for boots). Before you decide I am certifiable, please consider that we have not had a single epic meltdown in my house when a pint-size person desperately needs to find her "red plastic Little Bunny Foo Foo finger puppet" (true story), because she knows with utter certainty that the only possible place it could be, of course, is right there in Miscellaneous Hard Toys where it belongs.

As both a borderline hoarder and also a compulsive neat freak, another handy solution I've come up with is something I call "purgatory." If you went to Catholic school like me, you probably learned all about purgatory, which also was sometimes called "limbo," even though it's not nearly as fun as the dance with the same name. Purgatory/limbo was the middle ground between heaven and hell—not a bright and glorious paradise beyond comprehension but not a flaming pit of evil and suffering either—where babies went if they died before they were baptized. (Because of purgatory, when I was born more than a month premature and had to be rushed into emergency surgery, my mother put the lifesaving medical services on pause until she could enlist a priest to purge me of that pesky original sin I'd been born with. You know, so I could go to heaven. I am pretty sure I have undone her efforts by this point, but it was nice of her to try.)

Anyway, while Catholic purgatory was supposedly forever, my purgatory is only temporary. When I weed out a drawer or closet, there are always things I have no problem getting rid of. (Nyquil that expired in 2002? Buh-bye! Crevice attachment to the vacuum cleaner I replaced three years ago? See ya!) But the stuff that I'm on the fence about—like the platform boots that are super comfy and woefully out of style but might be useful for a costume party or killing a baseball-size spider—goes into a box, which I then seal with duct tape. I write the date and a list of the contents on the outside, should I actually get invited to that costume party (even though we both know I'll go out and buy or rent something cuter if I do) and then stuff it in my basement. If I haven't opened or thought about that box in a year, it goes to the first charity that will come and pick it up. Unopened. That last bit is critical, because if I take off the tape and go through it, invariably I'll get all nostalgic and try to sneak some of that shit right back into my closet. *So the box remains unopened.* Period.

Living in California, I have frequent opportunities to assess which of my possessions is indeed essential. These opportunities generally come in the form of massive out-of-control wildfires that like to race in the general direction of my house. Because our house sits at the tippy edge of some seriously rugged and undeveloped terrain that's prone to combusting, at least once a year we are under an evacuation watch or warning. When we get the call, my husband and I calmly go about the business of photographing any recent purchases or home improvements, locating our many animals, and readying our things to be loaded into our cars.

The first time this happened, we went a little bit apeshit. We gathered not just our priceless photos and important personal documents, but our computers and printers and the rest of our electronics. We took pictures from the walls and toys for the kids and, of course, our beloved pillows. I packed a year's worth of clothes I don't even necessarily like and toiletries for an army. When there was still some room in my SUV (because we packed both cars plus a trailer), I threw in a few more hampers full of clothes and shoes and DVDs and basically anything else that wasn't nailed down.

When the fire finally was contained and we were allowed back home, I looked at some of the crap I had packed. My computer, really? It's backed up remotely every night, and it's old and annoyingly slow and covered by my homeowners insurance and reconnecting it was a total nightmare, so that never got packed again. Ditto the wall art—except the originals painted by our friends and kids—and my old scuffed shoes. A very small part of me even fantasized about having to replace my wardrobe, because *next* time around I would go for quality over quantity, and I would stock my new closet with a handful of fabulous pieces—not just a bunch of shit that was on sale—and lots and lots of air.*

In *Lots of Candles, Plenty of Cake*, the brilliant Anna Quindlen speaks of a friend who has completely "forgone the entire era of crazed consumerism." Everything in this woman Susan's house, Quindlen writes, has a purpose, a point, or some profound meaning. She tells a particularly poignant story of one holiday when Susan and her husband allowed their children to open one gift each on Christmas Eve. The next morning, when the youngest saw his stack of presents beneath the tree, he responded with words I am certain I've never heard escape my own children's lips on Christmas morning (or my own, for that matter): "But I already have one."

---

* Yeah, right.

The thing is, I've read copious research that's found that stuff, in fact, does not make us happy—at least for long. The theory in technical terms is called hedonic adaptation, and essentially what it says is that after we get the things we yearn for the very most in this world, we revert to our pre-Jaguar/job/sexy-lover level of happiness within *three measly months.* It seems so improbable, and you are probably sitting there going, "Nope, not me! I'd be happy FOREVER if I had that stainless steel Viking under-counter wine refrigerator with the glass door!" But think about a time in your life when you were so miserably hot you thought you might pass out or die—and then how it felt when you hopped into that air-conditioned car or plunged into that icy pool. It was heavenly, right? And it continued to feel life-alteringly amazing for maybe three or four whole minutes before you got used to it and forgot all about your recent sticky, steamy misery. You adapted, you little hedonist, you. You didn't consciously set out to adapt or even give it a fleeting moment's thought while it was happening; it's just what you were hardwired to do.

According to this theory of hedonic adaptation, that huge raise you fantasize about getting, the one you're positive would completely change your life? If you landed that salary bump today and could fast-forward ninety days into the future, you might be disappointed to find that your mood and overall sense of well-being would be exactly zero percent greater than they are right this very minute. Ditto the mansion pinned to your vision board, the designer purse you're watching on eBay, and the tennis court you'd kill to build in the backyard. (If you win the lottery, you get a whole year to enjoy your ecstasy before going back to being just as giddy or miserable as you were before.)

Knowing that stuff doesn't make me happy is one thing; unloading much of the less-obvious excess is another. If I were being honest with myself, I would have to admit that there are several things—possibly tens of thousands of them, which are ridiculously organized and meticulously categorized, but still—in my house that absolutely, unequivocally should be donated or disposed of right this very instant. These include but are not limited to candles that have burned down to the little metal wick plate at the bottom (yes, the jar still smells delicious if I stick my nose down into it, but *come on*); the shampoo bottle that had one-sixteenth of an ounce of product left in it when I bought and immediately started using a re-placement; old toothbrushes (conceivably I *could* use these to scrub my grout, but I don't, and even if I did, one would suffice, so why do I have thirty-seven of them?); misfire makeup I've had for eons and never liked anyway (that stuff's only got a shelf life of about six months before it turns into a bacterial bachelor party); the manuals to appliances I no longer own—and even ones I do, because it's not like I ever need them, but if I did, I'm sure I could find them online; warped, sauce-stained Tupperware with missing lids; ripped underwear and stray, mateless socks; dozens of dry cleaning hangers idling limply under otherwise empty plastic; toys, games, and puzzles that are missing a critical part; and my children's baby teeth. (My mother saved all of mine in a plastic rain bonnet container and later gave them to me. Why do we do this? I think we can all agree that disengaged body parts are never, ever meant to be saved.*)

But there are other things that aren't so easily chucked. Letters from old boyfriends, my grade school uniform and high school cheerleading skirt, an art journal I kept in college, plans my dad drew for the bathroom my husband and I never added to the house we sold more than a decade ago, the positive pregnancy tests that were my first connections to my daughters.† I know that I should get rid of these things, because of that fire business and because Anna Quindlen would say it's the right thing to do, and also, if I keeled over tomorrow, it would be dropping the really shitty task of weeding through it all and deciding what to do with it into someone's (probably my sister Laurie's) lap.

But that's not how I'm wired. I'm an organized, sentimental fool. I like these tokens of the many could-be-forgotten moments in my life. They're comforting. Besides, announcing "I'm going to simplify this weekend" would be like proclaiming "I'm going to get my shit together by Thursday" if I were Lindsay Lohan. In other words, it's not going to happen.

Sorry, Laurie. And girls? I hope you're not as horrified as I was when I give you your teeth back.

---

* Goddamn it, I save my kids' teeth, too. And I can't throw them away. I've tried. This may be a cry for help.

† Yes, I kept a couple of sticks that I peed on. Wait. You didn't save these?

....

CHAPTER 5

I Don't Have Time for a Crisis (But I'll Have Another Drink)

I have a friend who likes to regale party guests with tales of his mother's raging alcoholism throughout his childhood. Apparently, the woman loved her scotch on the rocks and had a habit of asking her loved ones—very young children included—if they "wouldn't mind topping her off" and then offering up a bone-dry glass. Seems she'd make this request a dozen or more times an evening, generally until she passed out cold and her lifeless, drunken form had to be carted off to bed.

Hahahaha we all cackle collectively when we hear this story—topping her off!—because obviously she was a hard booze-drinking lushbag. The fact that we are all well into our fourth beer or third glass of wine when this story gets paraded

....

out doesn't seem relevant in the slightest. I mean, it's not like we're *alcoholics* or anything.

I was a heavy drinker in college, because who wanted to go to a frat party or campus bar perfectly sober? Besides, I was pretty sure that was what college was for: to sow your wild oats and get all of that overindulging out of your system while your system was still young enough to bounce back relatively quickly from the repeated abuse. We drank rotgut concoctions of whatever booze was cheap and plentiful at the moment (sometimes through a funnel and once out of a gigantic clean garbage can, I am not proud to admit) with a singular goal: to get drunk, fast. We even had a name for one of the premier benefits of our nightly binge drinking: the "shampoo effect." You know, because when you were still a tiny bit buzzed from the night before, you could get nice and liquored up that much faster.

Lather, rinse, repeat.

And then I grew up. Well, not really. But I graduated (with honors, somehow) and got a job (miraculously), and I realized that if I maintained my diligent seven-straight-nights-of-partying schedule, I could actually lose the aforementioned job and wind up living back at home with my parents. Which would be a total nightmare for countless reasons, one being that their liquor supply sucked unless you happened to fancy Southern Comfort and diet ginger ale or expired melon liqueur. So the new professional me drank strategically, reserving my nights out for when I knew I could be achingly, pukingly hungover the next day with a minimum of consequences.

At my second job,* I became close friends with an awesome lady named Michelle. I call her a "lady" because she was wise and mature at thirty-five, and I was a rather impulsive, slightly reckless twenty-five. In addition to being a lady, Michelle (who I am fortunate enough to call a dear friend to this day) was stone-cold cool. She was sleek and sophisticated and wore tortoiseshell glasses and *rode a fucking motorcycle* and smoked cigarettes and wore shoes that didn't come from Payless and had grown-up dinner parties. With vegetables and everything. None of my other friends were throwing dinner parties, I probably don't need to add. We ate frozen pizzas if we were home or happy hour appetizers if we were out.† I don't think I'd had a real, full-size meal that included anything green since I'd left for college until Michelle invited me over for one. Michelle was a young, modern-day Auntie Mame who served exotic cocktails out of matching glasses. Matching glasses! Can you imagine? The only glasses I had at the time may have been ones I accidentally walked out of a bar with.

Before long, Michelle and I were roommates.‡ She taught me to cook a few things, and overnight I had access to matching glasses whenever I wanted. We'd go out to a party or a bar

---

* I quit the first one because I landed the second one; I didn't get fired for smelling like tequila or plastering my ass cheeks to the office copy machine at the Christmas party and then forgetting about it, just so you know.

† We almost always cooked the pizzas, by the way.

‡ Not the kind who have sex even occasionally, not that there's anything wrong with that.

one or two nights a week, but on the other nights, my new roommate had the strangest habit I had ever seen: She'd come home from work, kick off her shoes, and enjoy a nice, cold beer or glass of chardonnay.

Just one.

"You going out tonight?" I remember asking once early on, vaguely hurt that I hadn't been invited.

"Nope," she'd replied breezily.

"Oh," I said. "Bad day?"

"Nope," she'd answered, taking a long, satisfying sip.

"Then why are you drinking?" I needed to know.

"I just like the taste," she'd said.

My still-young mind simply could not wrap itself around the idea of enjoying 130 or more calories of potentially mind-bending goodness simply for the taste. What was the point if you weren't out to catch a buzz, especially when you could have fifteen more French fries or two and a half cookies instead for the same amount of dietary damage? It was always about the buzz versus the calories (at least until around 1:30 in the morning when then it became *screw calories and I'm done drinking anyway, so let's go find an open drive-through,* but this will be covered in excruciating detail in a later chapter, I promise).

It would be another dozen or so years before I understood the lovely, magical, unwinding effect bestowed by a simple predinner cocktail. This epiphany happened to coincide with the exact moment I gave birth to my first child.

Even though she was a remarkably easy baby twenty-two hours out of the day, we called the window from five to seven p.m. the "witching hour." That's basically when she would scream inconsolably for no apparent reason, and no amount of rocking, bouncing, soothing, feeding, or pleading could make her stop.

"Getcha a glass of wine?" my husband Joe would shout over the wailing, running a hand through his frazzled hair.

"Dear God, yes, please," I'd yell back, wiping spit-up off my shoulder and staring at the clock.

By the time our daughter finally grew out of that hellish phase, the early evening cocktail habit had been firmly established. Now that we had something to be happy about (the lack of screaming coupled with the fact that I wasn't pregnant and could actually drink), the "witching hour" became regular old "happy hour." We agreed that since we both worked from home, we needed—no, we deserved—this gentle segue from the demands of our day jobs to the new madness that was the rest of our lives. Booze was a quitting time whistle, a pat on the back, a ten-minute chair massage, and a dangling carrot all at the same time. I'd look at my watch at 3:15 and automatically start calculating: an hour and forty-five minutes to go! Five o'clock couldn't come fast enough. And while the first pour rarely came long after that precise and carefully chosen time, it never, ever came before it. Because everyone knows that only alcoholics drink during the day.

Besides, I was a wine girl and alcoholics downed hard liquor. Did you ever see a bum swigging out of a paper-bag-wrapped bottle of Cabernet? Me neither. That's because wine is classy. It's social. You don't have to hide it. Little old ladies drink it at lunch. Fancy restaurants have separate phonebook-size menus dedicated to it. Rich people build entire temperature-controlled subterranean shrines to house it. To speak of it intelligently requires at least a passing knowledge of French language and pronunciation (Bordeaux, Beaujolais, Cabernet, Viognier), and honestly—what's more refined than that?

(Next time you see a plastered panhandler, try this: *"Bonjour, mon ami. Belle journée, n'est-ce pas? Comment vous sentez-vous aujourd'hui?"* I'll give you fifty bucks if he replies in the most romantic of all languages or even doesn't spit at you.)

Even though I very much like to drink, I don't like being drunk. That whole room-spinning thing just freaks me out, and most days I'd rather be wrapped in a blanket of thorns and asked to deliver an eleven-pound baby than endure a searing hangover. For these reasons, I reserve my one big blowout night of the year for my annual girls' trip. This is a long weekend I take every year with four or seven (depending on the year and who's knocked up/getting married/getting divorced/remodeling her kitchen) of my closest lifetime girlfriends. I have known most of these women—each more successful, professional, and amazing than the next—since the siphoning-grain-alcohol-from-a-trashcan days, and it's almost inevitable that there will be a bender. We drink totally responsibly,* laugh until our faces hurt, and take lots of pictures of ourselves sprawled out in our inebriated still-got-it glory. We

---

* Meaning: We take cabs, stay together, and don't let anybody do anything irreversibly stupid.

do this because we can and because we can't do it at home even though we wouldn't want to anyway. We do it to feel young and carefree again, because on the parts of the trip when we're not plastered or getting pedicures, we talk about our dying (or dead) parents and our exhausting kids and our recent biopsies and our falling faces and our maddening husbands and *their* confusing and unfathomable midlife crises. We do it to celebrate the fact that we've kept our shit together for the previous mind-blowing 364 days in a row, and we do it because it's really fucking fun.

For a million reasons—the rarely getting drunk outside of my girls' weekend part, the not hiding my drinking part, the fact that I am an adult and can do what I want—I rarely gave my alcohol consumption a second thought. Until right around forty. That's when some tiny farmer snuck into my brain and planted a few robust seeds of doubt. Did I drink too much? Could I stop if I wanted to? Did I have a, you know, problem? Sure, I'd gone sauce free when I was pregnant—but hadn't I brought a nice bottle of wine to the hospital in my postpartum tote both times to enjoy immediately after delivery? All of my friends drank exactly as much as I did. Did that mean I *didn't* have a problem, or was it more that I had intentionally surrounded myself with likeminded imbibers, which obviously would be the sign of a problem? For the record, I wasn't pounding a few bottles a night; I'm talking two, three glasses of wine over a four-hour period. I barely ever felt a hint of a buzz, so it was a marvel even to me how much I looked forward to wine o'clock.

"Do you think we drink too much?" I'd ask my friends at our semiregular happy hour gatherings.

"Probably," any one of them would reply, topping off everyone's empty glasses.

The thoughts persisted. Every once in a while, I'd make a bold declaration but only to myself: *I'm not going to drink tomorrow*, I'd announce silently. You know, just to prove that I could go a whole day without it. And then five o'clock would roll around—predictably the way it always does, which is exactly when I'm jonesing for a drink—and the excuse tap would start flowing: *You know what? It's not like I have anything to prove. Alcohol isn't a problem for me. I don't drink to get drunk, it doesn't negatively affect my life at home or work, and I'd never drink and drive. Plus I work hard and I'm an awesome mom and I did all of those lousy chores today on top of it all! I earned a drink or two, damn it! I'll not drink tomorrow, really that's a much better idea anyway. Besides, I can stop anytime I want to. It just so happens that I don't feel like stopping right at this exact moment. In fact, what I really want is a glass of wine. Honey, would you mind topping me off?*

"My Welcome-to-Midlife Moment Was . . ."

When I realized that more than one margarita in an hour gives me a headache.

—MELISSA

A gal I know who also likes to enjoy a nightly glass or two of the grape was telling me recently about an episode in her house. She'd run out of wine,* so without thinking anything of it, she opened a brand-new bottle of vodka and fixed herself a cocktail. When she was done with the fixing part, she pushed the vodka bottle into the exact same spot on the kitchen counter that her ubiquitous bottle of wine would otherwise have occupied.

"What the hell is this?" her husband said immediately when he spotted the vodka bottle.

"Oh, we were out of wine, so I opened some vodka," she explained.

"Well, why is it out on the *counter?*" he wanted to know. The man was aghast, horrified even.

"Because I might have another one," she said simply.

He was having none of her silly logic. Instead, and even though he'd never once in more than two decades minded having an opened bottle of wine on the counter, he promptly stashed that liquor bottle away and out of sight—even though they were the only ones at home—and you know why as well as I do: because *wine is classy* while booze smacks of smelly, desperate old ladies wearing dirty housedresses and talking to themselves while pushing rusty shopping carts.

My friend and I laughed about the whole episode merrily,

---

* Obviously, she's a rookie.

because it's *not like we were alcoholics*. Not long afterward, though, a funny thing happened as I was sitting down to dinner with my family.

"Oh my gosh, Mom!" shouted my then seven-year-old.

"What's wrong, honey?" I asked.

"Where's your wine?" she demanded. She actually sounded a little panicked, bless her tiny, innocent little heart.

I'd merely left my glass on the counter by the stove where I'd been cooking. It's not like I'd forsaken it completely or anything. But the mere fact that my youngest daughter immediately recognized the missing beverage *and reacted with unfettered alarm* made me feel like maybe it was time to take a little break. The last thing I wanted was her sitting around someday drinking Southern Comfort and diet ginger ale or expired melon liqueur with her friends—because everything always comes full circle, doesn't it?—and talking about her winoholic mom.

"I'm not going to drink during the week anymore," I announced to Joe later, when the kids were out of earshot.

"Okay, I'll do it with you," he said easily. I thought that the fact that he didn't ask why or even try to argue the idea might be some sort of sign.

"Oh, wait," he said suddenly. "What about Thursday?" Thursday is his basketball night, which consists of an hour and a half of sweaty hooping followed by three or five hours of beer pounding. It's the highlight of his week, his one chance to unwind without me nagging the living hell out of him (well, honestly), and I wouldn't dream of taking it away from him, even just the boozing part.

....

"You can drink on Thursday," I conceded generously.

"Okay," he said, relieved. "Oh, wait. But what about Sunday? Does Sunday count as a weekday or weekend? Because we have a lot of barbecues on Sundays."

"I think it could go either way," I admitted, watching our nondrinking "weeknights" dwindle. "Do you think you could do Monday through Wednesday?" I said this a tiny bit sarcastically.

"Totally," he said.

"Okay, I'm doing Monday through Thursday," I declared.

The first few weeks, I have to tell you, were a bitch. I had a searing, around-the-clock headache, which is odd because that sounds like a symptom of withdrawal or something, and it's *not like I was an alcoholic.* The singular hour from five to six was the worst, survived only by consuming tumbler after tumbler of lemonade. ("Your teeth might rot out, but at least your liver will still be functioning," Joe joked. Hardy-fucking-har.)

" My Welcome-to-Midlife Moment Was . . . "

When I realized I can't read the martini choices unless the menu is at least four feet from my face.

—KT

A few weeks into my new semidry lifestyle, a friend invited me over for a cocktail. My younger daughter has an evening gymnastics class in this friend's neighborhood, and we'd often connect to kill the two hours. But it was on a Wednesday.

"I'm not drinking during the week anymore," I admitted.

"Ugh," she said. "I say *all the time* that I'm going to do that . . . but I never do."

"Me, too!" I screamed. "I couldn't even do it for a single night! I had to go the whole week. It sort of sucks."

"How long have you been doing it?" she wanted to know.

"Less than a month," I told her.

"Do you feel a lot better?" she asked.

"Nope," I admitted. "Not at all."

"Crap," she said. "Okay, I'm going to do it, too."

"Do you still want to get together and not drink on Wednesday?" I asked.

"I guess," she said, defeated.

We wound up totally rearranging her living room furniture that night, including moving a three-hundred-pound rug that had landed in its current spot years ago and been deemed too heavy to move ever again. When we finished, panting and sweating, the room was transformed. We marveled at how much you could get done in an hour and a half when you weren't doing one-arm biceps curls with a goblet. (Then we lamented how nice it would have been to toast ourselves and our kickass efforts with an oversized glass of something deliciously fermented. Sigh.)

I began mentioning my Wineless Weekday routine to other friends as the subject came up—generally when I was invited somewhere where it would be obvious I was going to be the lone teetotaler.

"Um, yeah, sure, I'd love to come," I'd say, "but I'm not drinking during the week."

"Why?" they always asked.

"I don't know," I'd say. "I was thinking maybe I drink too much."

"Oh, that, right," they all said.

"Do you feel better when you don't drink?" they wanted to know.

"Not really," I admitted.

"We're going to do it, too!" they said, one after another. Some of them actually did.

As for me and Joe, we've been pretty good about staying dry during the week, breaking the pact only on either highly celebratory or super-stressful evenings, like the one where I had to explain to our sweet, innocent children how our unneutered male dog could possibly have knocked up the neighborhood bitch when they *weren't even married*. If that doesn't earn you a goddamned glass of wine on a designated nondrinking night, I don't know what does.

CHAPTER 6

On Miniskirts and Mom Jeans

In my twenties, I worked in New York City at various magazines. Just like the things you see *in* magazines frequently aren't anything you might encounter in real life, so it goes with what you see *at* magazines. Forty-year-old women would come to work wearing crotch-skimming silver pleather skirts that stuck straight out from the waist to reveal sequined hot pants beneath. Fifty-year-olds would sport leopard leggings and red stilettos (and not in an ironic Peg Bundy sort of way). Sixty-year-olds flounced down the halls in dresses made entirely of hot pink faux fur. For a while, when the sexy-schoolgirl look was all the rage, every one of my female colleagues, no matter her age, occasionally and unapologetically came to the office in over-the-knee socks paired with a plaid pleated mini. I'm just glad I got out of that industry before whale tails* and Crocs were things.

The irony here is that these were all *fashion* magazines—the very ones who dedicate reams of paper every year telling their readers precisely how to "Dress [Their] Age!"

The thing about age-appropriate dressing, the magazines explain, is that when you fail to do it, you're announcing to the world that you are sad and insecure and trying desperately to cling to your too-distant youth.† (As if the Botox that might kill us and the cars we can't afford and the fact that we're all suddenly training for triathlons and mud runs weren't dead giveaways.) According to folks who profess to be experts on this shit, donning a "classic sheath dress or tailored pair of slacks or fabulous statement necklace" (slacks and statement necklaces!) on the other hand apparently conveys sexy confidence. Silly me, I thought your attitude did that.

Every fashion magazine and website geared to anyone old enough to have seen *Dallas* in primetime frequently features articles detailing the so-called "rules for dressing your age." Each article contradicts the last, of course, because they rely on different "experts" who all have very definitive and varying opinions on the subject. On any given day, the "rules" may or may not include: nothing from the juniors department after

---

* That's what you call a thong poking up and out of the back of your jeans. I did not know that term until now. This is probably because I'm old.

† Unless you work for the magazine in question, in which case *obviously* you are immune to rules of any kind.

thirty, no shorty-shorts after forty, nothing above the knee after fifty, and no jeans after sixty. Oh, and comfort before couture (mostly), sweats are for the gym, less is more, size doesn't matter, and don't forget to accessorize!

One website I found dedicated entirely to what to wear after forty offered a handy list of items to avoid at all costs, which I will summarize for you here:

- Daisy Dukes
- brightly colored cowboy boots
- crotch-skimming dresses
- crotch-skimming skirts
- pleated, peg-leg "mom jeans"
- ripped jeans
- ill-fitting blazers
- anything that produces camel-toe
- ratty sweats
- too-long skirts

I don't understand this list at all. First of all, does the author mean to imply that there's another age group out there who *can* pull off ill-fitting blazers and mom jeans and pants that produce camel-toe? And what's a "too-long" skirt, anyway? One that's dragging on the ground collecting rocks and leaves and small, unattended children? Wouldn't a "too *anything*" article of clothing (too tight, too loose, too ugly, too cheaply made, too out of style, too Ed Hardy) automatically make any Don't list? And what on earth is wrong with brightly colored cowboy boots? I have a hot pink pair that kicks ass, lady, and I'd buy them in red and turquoise, too, if they made them and they wouldn't break the bank. (The same site bans "animal prints and disco fabrics," and I can only assume they mean wearing them *together*, because who doesn't love zebra stripes and sequins?) This list reminds me of whenever I read things about my astrological sign. "Taureans are stubborn and love nice things," the description always reads. Is there a sign notorious for being pushovers who love crap?

Another website offers this handy set of guidelines: "Be sure to always highlight the most beautiful part about yourself, and cover up parts you're not so fond of. If you have beautiful legs, a smooth neckline or nice cleavage, be sure to show it off but always leave something to the imagination. In return, 'hide' unattractive body parts such as flabby upper arms, a double chin, a wrinkled décolleté or saggy knees. In these cases, stay away from sleeveless or caped sleeves, avoid wearing tight necklaces and exposing necklines (wear fashionable scarfs [sic] instead), and knee-length skirts with darker pantyhose."

I am not positive, but I think that if I followed this advice, I'd be showing up to school pickup today wearing a turtleneck and tights under my burka.

" My Welcome-to-Midlife Moment Was . . . "

When I found something cute at Chico's.

—CM

In the celebitchy magazines I like to devour at the hair salon, impossibly hot Carmen Electra has been bashed for going backless after forty (and if Carmen can't pull it off, who on earth can?), stunning Heidi Klum's gotten verbally spanked for dressing like an eighteen-year-old (I say if she still has the body of one, she's allowed!), Melanie Griffith—at fifty-four— has been told she is a solid fourteen years past her prime legging-wearing days, and Lisa Rinna's been scolded for busting out of a top "she may have bought when she was on *Melrose Place.*" Apparently, Madonna shouldn't be allowed out of her house at all anymore, at least until she agrees to put away the cheerleading skirts and bubble dresses. Supposed style pros have held up lovely Kylie Minogue as proof that denim jumpsuits are okay for toddlers but not quadragenarians and admonished gorgeous Halle Berry, who was very busy rocking a formfitting, almost demure silver dress at the time, saying "just because you *can* wear something doesn't mean you should."

It *doesn't*?

In the incriminating photos accompanying all of the above alleged fashion don'ts, I would like to point out that every one of these women look amazing. Phenomenally, annoyingly, cloyingly, impossibly amazing. (Except maybe Rinna, but I'm going to give her the benefit of the doubt and assume she was mid-jog when the paparazzi's shutter snapped, and that's why her top boobs were busting out of her otherwise perfectly suitable workout cami.)

My tastes haven't changed much in the past two decades, and subsequently, neither has my wardrobe. To an extent I mean that literally; I still own some of the better pieces I wore to my *Seventeen* magazine job in 1993. And yes, I occasionally wear the more timeless ones, including a black Nicole Miller cocktail dress, a Calvin Klein pencil skirt, and a Max Azria cape. Never mind that you might find all of these things on a "vintage" rack at the flea market. They're cute, they're classic, they're great quality, they still fit, and I'm not getting rid of them.

I get the dressing-your-age bit in vague, generalized theory; nobody wants to (or should have to) see yards of flaccid flesh squished into the skimpy denim cutoffs and backless halter tops my daughters pine for (and look ridiculously fantastic in). But what about the things that are stylish and trendy at any given moment and *don't* show an excess of skin, like skinny jeans and leather skirts and lace or neon or whatever they're hawking in the fashion magazines at the time? Are those okay? Or am I supposed to stick with the mom uniform (where I live it's designer yoga pants and a matching tech tank and jacket or jeans and a black or white tee) for the next twenty or so years and then segue straight into polyester pants and caftans?

Maybe it's because I work at home, often in my PJs until I have to pick up my kids from school, or maybe it's because I just don't give a flying fuck, but I am pretty sure that I don't dress my age. I feel confident about this because my fashion-obsessed ten-year-old tries to borrow my clothes all the time. (She hasn't yet hit that notorious age where the mere fact that I own or wear something makes it permanently and irrevocably uncool. And in my defense, I never, *ever* try to borrow her clothes.) I still shop in the junior department sometimes, because usually the stuff there is cuter and cheaper.

I have to say, it's not really my fault. My kids have Tilly's and Justice, and my mom has Lands' End and Coldwater Creek. I can find jeans at Nordstrom or the occasional top at Macy's, but what's out there that's *just for me*?

Other than no longer feeling like a super-deep V-neck is my best friend or ally, the biggest change in the way I dress as I've gotten older* has happened below my ankles. When shopping for shoes as a younger woman, my only concerns were a) how insufferably adorable they were, and b) if I could afford them. Period. If a pair of shoes met these simple criteria, it made no difference if they pinched, pulled, caused torturous cramping, or even drew blood after a few painful steps. I strapped those suckers to my feet, stuffed my purse with a stash of Band-Aids, and went my painful way. These days, before venturing out for an evening, I have to have this conversation with my husband:

ME: *[considering a pair of strappy stilettos]* Can we valet park?

JOE: *[looking at me like I'm batshit crazy]* There's a parking garage two blocks from the restaurant.

ME: *[looking longingly at the stilettos]* So no?

JOE: Why would you own a pair of shoes that you can't even walk *two blocks* in?

---

* Notice I didn't say "as I've gotten *more mature*."

ME: [holds up the amazing shoes in question in reply]
JOE: [shakes head sadly]

I used to laugh when my mom would carry bedroom slippers in her purse when she went out (this was before they made those foldable ballet flats that Oprah loves and that were created for just this purpose). Now I get it. I don't stash slippers in my bag; that would be hitting way too close to home. But I do stow a cute pair of gold Havaianas flip-flops in my car for those occasions when I'd rather gnaw my own foot off at the ankle than take another miserable step in a pair of heels.

Although when I buy new shoes I now insist that they be comfortable from the get-go (no more of that "breaking them in" business—who has the time or energy for that?), until recently I still had dozens of pairs that were excruciating even to look at. "I might wear these when we go to our Japanese friends' house for dinner because you have to take your shoes off at the door when you go there" is how I justified keeping them, an argument that would be relatively solid if we actually had Japanese friends who might invite us over for a shoeless meal.

Shoes are different than clothes, of course. They don't generally look fabulous on you one month and appalling the next. You rarely catch a glimpse of your reflection in a store window and think, "Oh my GOD, I'm Sasquatch and nobody told me!" And we rarely if ever say to our friends, "Be honest. Do these shoes make my feet look fat?"

Still, I decided this past weekend to go through the embarrassment that is my shoe collection and get rid of anything that no longer served me or my needs. Among the items that didn't make the final cut were at least six pairs of heels that hurt before I even tried standing up in them, three mateless flip-flops, and one pair that consisted of two left shoes. (I swear it. I'm almost positive that I owned two complete sets at one point, but the whereabouts of those two wayward righties are anyone's guess.) I wound up with two huge garbage bags of castoffs and a whole lot of freed-up closet space. I walked around high on accomplishment all weekend.

"You should do the rest of your closet," Joe suggested gently.

"Never should on anyone else, and don't let anyone should on you," I scolded him.

A lot of women I know do seem to think that midlife is a good time to take stock of your wardrobe. You know, now that you're probably done having babies and your body has more or less settled into the size it wants to be (which may not be the size *you* want it to be, but that's another book altogether), and hopefully, you've figured out what looks good on you and amassed enough money to buy a few decent staples. But I honestly wouldn't even know where to start. If I went by the rule "if you wouldn't keep it if you won the lottery, you shouldn't keep it at all," I'd have about four things left out of the four thousand I own.

My pal Chris said her purging started with a "come to Jesus" conversation she had with herself after trying on every last thing in her closet searching for something suitable to wear to work one day and finding that the majority of it didn't fit, was woefully out of style, or was otherwise just *wrong*.

"I had jeans ranging from size zero to size fourteen in every color of the rainbow," Chris confessed. "I was hanging on to the ones that were too small hoping I'd fit back into them someday and keeping the ones that were too big . . . just in case. But I realized that if I lose or gain any amount of weight, I know I'll just go out and buy something new, so I took the whole lot to Goodwill."

Another pal, a former corporate exec named Ellie who gave up her high-powered career to stay home and raise her kids and never went back, said she could no longer stand seeing the brigade of power suits idling in her closet. "It was like they were taunting me for my decision not to work," Ellie explained. "Plus I paid a bloody fortune for them. So I loaded up my trunk and brought them to a consignment shop." Unfortunately, the snotty shop owner informed Ellie that her twenty-year-old suits were—wait for it—about twenty years out of style.

"They are?" Ellie asked the consignment lady incredulously, fingering the designer fabric and feeling simultaneous pangs of nostalgia and regret.

"When did shoulder pads go out of style?" she asked me later.

"I think it was right about the time *The Nanny* went off the air," I told her.

"And double-breasted suits are out, too?" she wanted to know.

"Pretty much," I said gently.

"But won't they come back in again?" she asked hopefully.

With some gentle nudging, Ellie eventually decided that saving her outdated designer work wardrobe for an occasional costume party was a ridiculous notion and donated the mess to Dress for Success. They were almost as elated to have it as she was to finally get rid of it.

If there *is* a secret to dressing my age, I can sum it up in one word: Spanx. If you don't know what Spanx are, please put this book down, cup your hands around your mouth, and bellow at the top of your lungs, "WOULD SOMEBODY PLEASE MOVE THE VERY LARGE ROCK THAT IS BLOCKING THE ENTRANCE TO MY CAVE SO I CAN CRAWL OUT FOR THE FIRST TIME THIS MILLENNIUM?" While you wait, I'll enlighten you: Spanx are supersleek, turbocharged scraps of magically engineered fabric that suck everything in and up without any ugly stitching or painful whale bones digging into your flesh. Fine, they're girdles. *But these are not your grandma's girdles, okay?* (They're also not repackaged duct tape, I swear.) The Spanx tagline is "the secret to lightweight slimming," but for me, it's not even about slimming. Hate me if you will, but I'm not trying to look skinny. It's more that I'd like to look less *skin-y*, because I seem to have far more epidermal casing than I need to hold all of my organs in place. But when I slip into my Spanx, it's like somebody has sprayed me with a shrink-wrap coating that tucks everything in and holds it there. *Without tape.*

You want to know how good Spanx are? Founder Sara Blakely recently was named the planet's youngest self-made female billionaire by *Forbes* magazine and tapped as one of

Time's 100 Most Influential People. IN THE WORLD. (Yes, a lady who cut the legs off her pantyhose to make an invisible girdle and then turned the idea into an empire is on a global who's-who list that includes economists, activists, senators, Rihanna, Tim Tebow, and *Mashable*'s Pete Cashmore.) In addition to an exhaustive selection of tummy-taming, thigh-trimming, butt-boosting shapewear, Spanx now makes everything from yoga pants and workout skirts to dresses, swimsuits, and even socks. (In case your friend tells you that your tennis shoes do in fact make your feet look fat.) The only problem with any of it, as far as I can see, is that eventually you have to take that shit off and face what lies beneath. But if you have any plans to wear white pants or a fitted dress ever again, I highly recommend sucking it up. Literally and figuratively.

In a recent issue of *Allure* magazine, writer Simon Doonan addressed the whole dress-your-age business. "There is nothing more annoying than the idea of age-appropriate rules and regulations," Doonan insisted. "As far as I am concerned you can wear whatever you want and at any age. All you need is conviction." And more than likely, a drawer full of Spanx.

CHAPTER 7

Damn You, Middle-Age Spread

Here's a fun experiment: Stop any random middle-aged woman on the street and ask her how she feels about her weight. (You might want to duck after you do this because there's a decent chance you'll get clocked in the face just for asking.) Odds are she is not happy about it one little bit. She might blame menopause or hormones or her scale or the fact that she has "no time to exercise,"* but regardless of the perceived culprit, you can bet your ever-widening ass she's fighting that woefully termed reality known as middle-age spread.

I know this because I am an expert on all things related to

---

* Her constantly updated Facebook page may suggest otherwise, but you'd be wise to let this go.

weight. Not that I have any formal training on the subject, but if you could earn advanced degrees through painful, humiliating experience—which I totally think you should—I would have a PhD in dieting. I've alternately existed for weeks at a stretch on nothing but sausage, cabbage soup, cottage cheese, macadamia nuts, Slimfast, and pasta marinara. (Remember the carbs-are-your-friend-but-fat-makes-you-fat era? Damn, that was my favorite.) I've popped questionable pills that made my heart race, pedaled to Japan and back on a stationary bike, and stocked my cupboards with fat-free, sugar-free, chemical-laden, cardboard-like "substitutes" for everything edible. After all of this, I have come to the very scientific conclusion that dieting sucks.

Ironically, I was a scrawny slip of a kid. In fact, my nickname growing up was "No Body." Get it? Because I had *no body.* Hahahaha except *hello, moronic adults in my life, did you ever stop to think that to my ears you were calling me NOBODY?* Fortunately, in my teens, I read a book about animal cruelty and became a "vegetarian." This was an odd and surprising choice by all accounts, seeing as there wasn't a single vegetable I would actually eat, if you didn't count the nearly nutritionally devoid iceberg lettuce, and only then if it was smothered in a gallon of French dressing. Being a vegetarian was great because I got to eat pasta every single day! And pizza. And bagels. And French fries. (I convinced my mom potatoes were a vegetable using the airtight "they grow in the ground" argument, and because we were from New York City and didn't know much about farming and also because there was no Internet to use for fact-checking purposes, she was sort of forced to believe me.) Now that I could never, ever have a delectable bite of corned beef or crispy strip of bacon again, I consoled myself with a bottomless bowl of buttered noodles.

The funniest thing happened when I became a vegetarian: I got fat. At least nobody called me No Body anymore.

College didn't help. There I was with my new extra padding and no parental supervision when I met my two new best friends: Binge Drinking and her pal late-night Drunken Gorging. I shudder to calculate my daily collegiate consumption of booze from a caloric standpoint, and don't even get me started on the nightly macaroni-pizza-nacho orgies that followed the partying. I was aware of the fact that I was fat (my dad made a helpful point of mentioning it whenever I came home, in case I hadn't noticed), and I did not like it one bit. But I also *really* liked eating and drinking. What was a girl supposed to do?

One of my party buddies at the time was a girl named Melanie. Like me, Mel had been diligently working to pack on the requisite Freshman Fifteen, and also like me, she was an overachiever. Then Mel went home for three weeks for the holiday break and came back twenty pounds lighter. *How in the hell had she lost what amounted to a pound a day,* the rest of us demanded to know. Apparently, her mom had taken her to some famous Miami Beach fat-fighting guru, who had explained that if she merely jabbed herself in the gut with his magical solution a few times a day, she could continue to drink and eat like a competitive wrestler and any extra weight would just magically fall right off. (Our roommate insisted she didn't know what was in those syringes, but the rumor was they were filled with a disgusting concoction involving amphetamines and liquefied human placenta.) And it worked. Mel continued to eat (jab!) and drink (stab!) and party (prick!) along with the rest of us (poke!) and I'll be damned if she didn't keep losing weight (thrust!). That impossibly skinny bitch paraded around campus in tiny shorts and went out in skintight Robert Palmer–backup-singer dresses (this was the '80s), and it was really hard not to hate her.

We didn't have to hate her for long. One sad day for poor Mel, those shots just stopped working. The weight started to creep back on. No matter how many times she stabbed herself with her bottomless stash of needles, it wouldn't stop. By the end of that year, Mel had gained back all of the weight she'd lost plus another few pounds for good measure.

So if injecting ourselves with fetomaternal organs on speed wasn't the answer, how were all of these other gals in our dorm—many of whom ate and drank and partied heartily right alongside us—staying so skinny? Apparently, I was told, a lot of them just excused themselves to the bathroom after a meal or a bender, jammed a slender finger down their elegant throats, and ridded themselves of all of those pesky calories. I decided to give it a go once after a big night of porking out. It was horrific. I nearly choked to death and my eyes watered for about an hour afterward and my throat felt like I'd swallowed a gallon of battery acid. Still, I tried it a few more times, thinking maybe I just needed some practice. But bulimic I was not meant to be.

Sophomore year my friends and I went to the Florida Keys

for spring break. I watched nubile-bodied girls my age running around in bikinis and felt stabs of jealousy and anger, feelings I numbed with epic quantities of food and booze. The trip turned out to be a blast, in the drunken-blur sense at least. And then I saw the pictures.

Wow, that's a really bad picture! I thought, standing at the drugstore counter and sifting through the pile. *I look really fat there. And there, too. Holy cow, I'm burning this one! This one, too. OMG, I'm burning ALL of these.*

I'd known that I wasn't exactly skinny, but was I really *that fat*?

I decided right then and there that I had had enough. I would go on a diet. I would eat nothing but big green salads with fat-free dressing and drink sparkling water until I lost the weight. I could do this. I *would* do this. I wanted it that badly. *Nothing I ate could taste as good as being skinny would feel.* (I actually saw that for the first time on a *Saturday Night Live* skit. Obviously, I knew they were mocking something, but I remember thinking *that's actually sort of brilliant! I should re-member that.*) Sure, it would be a sacrifice. But the payoff! Oh, the beautiful, enviable payoff! I was as committed as a girl could be.

I can't remember if that one lasted five minutes or ten.

It turned out, this dieting business was a bitch. While I had never really given much thought to food or calories before, suddenly those two things consumed my every waking thought. I thought about what I was going to eat and what I wasn't going to eat and what I should have eaten, and I beat myself up for every forbidden forkful. I bought fat-free cheese and crackers and cookies and chips by the trunkload and munched on them around the clock. They all tasted like crap, but I ate them anyway because they were *fat-free* and I wanted to be that! Never hungry but never satisfied, I'd eat and eat and eat, all the while mentally calculating calories and fat grams and promising to do better the next day.

Getting dressed was torture. "Does this make me look fat?" my roommates and I would ask each other as we tried on slouchy black outfit after outfit. None of us had the balls to reply with the truth: "No, honey. Your *FAT* makes you look fat." I became a math whiz, able to calculate any dish's dietary damage on sight. I hated every second of it. *I am starting a new diet tomorrow!* was my last waking thought on any given drunken evening. Then I'd wake up hungover, and everybody knows the saying: Starve a cold, feed a hangover. Preferably something fried.

I happened to live in the athletic dorm, which was another irony because I had never played a sport in my life. I had never watched a single football game or tennis match on TV either, and I couldn't even toss a Frisbee. But I'd turned in my college registration paperwork late, and all of the campus dorms were full, so my parents were forced to fork over for the pricey private dorm, the one where all of the athletes lived. Gabby Reece—yes, the achingly gorgeous volleyball phenom/glamazon/supermodel—lived on my floor. I'd watch her stride through the cafeteria with her perfect, gazelle-like body day after day and marvel at the fact that we were even both the same species. I'd heard she was friendly and approachable, but I wasn't about to find out for myself. Who wanted to get caught standing next to *that*? And then one day, admiring Gabby's obnoxiously perfect abs while she frolicked in our dorm pool while my friends and I drank beer and refused to take off our cover-ups, it hit me: I should work out!

Why hadn't I thought of it before? I would just work out and get skinny and toned like Gabby, and life would be great. I joined the local gym and became a recognized-by-name regular. Sometimes I'd do three aerobics classes back-to-back— trying in vain to undo the caloric damage I'd done the night before (or preempt the similar destruction I knew I'd inflict later that day). *I'll bet Gabby Reece doesn't eat half a pizza at 2 a.m.*, I'd scold myself after a binge. *Fuck you*, myself would reply. *I worked out today. Pass me another slice.*

Working out did not help me lose weight.

The fact that I was constantly "on a diet" (that "never worked") didn't seem all that odd to me. It was just the way it was. My mom had been on the same diet for as long as I could remember. Her weight never, ever changed, but every day of my life I had heard a detailed account of her efforts to shed those *last ten pounds*. Apparently, they were stubborn little SOBs.

My junior year in college I signed up for a semester at la Sorbonne in Paris.* The very first thing I noticed when I got

---

* I was minoring in French, a degree that it turns out comes in extremely handy for nobody, ever.

off of the plane was how impossibly, insanely thin French women are. Not just in general; I'm talking *every single one of them*. Finding a fat Frenchwoman is harder than finding an employee on the floor of Costco when you can't figure out where the hell they decided to move the dried mango slices and cat food this week.

The French must be genetically superior, I thought. That was all there was too it. They had to be—because these women ate like linebackers! Croissants and crepes and everything a la crème. Day after day I'd sit in cafés and watch these spaghetti-thin genetic freaks dip their big, crusty chunks of baguette in bowls of olive oil and eat the fattiest meats on the planet— steak and duck and sausage swimming in buttery *beurre blanc*—without guilt or consequence. Meanwhile, I couldn't find a single fat-free cracker in the entire country.

Finally I figured it out: It was the wine! See, I was eating exactly what they were eating—well, minus the butter and delicious sauces and in grotesque portions—but like an ignorant American, I was washing it down with *beer.* Silly me! I switched from Budweiser to Bordeaux and waited for the weight to fall off. You will be shocked to learn that it did not happen.

I came back to the States with special souvenirs of my time in France. I brought them with me everywhere I went. They're called haunches.

After graduation, I got my first job. It was a really glamorous gig in advertising sales, and by "glamorous" I mean "whatever the diametric opposite of glamorous is." I'd check into my tiny cubicle in the morning, map out my day's route, and then hit the road, dashing from one client to the next in the hopes that one of those bastards would spring for a full-page, full-color ad so I could pay my rent and maybe buy myself some new boots. In case you've never worked in sales, I'll let you in on a secret: Sales is really another word for "schmoozing," and one typically schmoozes one's clients over a meal.

Faced daily with restaurant lunch menus that didn't feature SnackWell's cookies or Baked Lays and dining partners I didn't want to make uncomfortable with a litany of sauces-on-the-side requests, I was forced to consume real food. I ate soup with croutons in it, turkey sandwiches with cheese and may-onnaise, and salads with bacon bits and olive oil dressing. (I'd long since abandoned my pretend vegetarianism.) I ate bread with butter (not fake butter spread!) and slices of avocado and spicy, peanut buttery Pad Thai. Man, I'd forgotten how good food could taste. In the back of my mind, I was sure I was going to balloon up like a Macy's Thanksgiving Day Parade float, but I was too busy—and too satisfied—to care.

The most incredible thing ever happened when I stopped dieting: I lost weight. You can't imagine how crazy it was to discover that for the first time in my adult life, I wasn't con-sciously restricting or analyzing every morsel I put in my mouth—in fact, I was eating *whatever the hell I wanted*—and I had *lost weight*. I wondered if maybe I'd finally managed to get myself a tapeworm. I decided not to get it checked, because if I did have a tapeworm, the doctors would most certainly want to remove it, and then I'd gain the weight right back, just like poor Mel had.

I got downright skinny. A college friend came to visit me and told me she was worried about me because she could see my spine. I tried to hide my pride. Other friends would ask me how I'd done it—which diet I had used—and nobody believed me when I told them my Big Secret was that I'd stopped dieting. And that when I had, I had completely stopped obsessing about food. And that when I'd stopped obsessing about food, I didn't need to eat around the clock. That after I'd had a simple, satisfying meal, I could get on with my life—which turned out to be quite full when there was room for something in it besides thoughts of forbidden food.

I stayed skinny for twenty years, even after gaining fifty pregnancy pounds—twice—and popping out what I think we can all agree were unnaturally massive babies at nine pounds apiece.* I ate whatever I wanted, stopped when I was full, and pretty much assumed I'd won the war with food.

"Enjoy it while you can," older friends warned me, "because your metabolism is going to screech to a halt the day you turn forty."

Not my super-metabolism, I'd think smugly, popping another sweet potato fry into my mouth. *I've got this thing figured out.*

And then I turned forty. I kept right on doing what I'd been doing all along, namely eating burgers and fries and bread

---

* Newborn babies, in my opinion, ought to be about six pounds, seven max. Nine pounds is creeping into Thanksgiving turkey territory.

dipped in olive oil whenever the urge struck—in mostly modest, satisfying portions of course—and drinking my coffee with generous amounts of half-and-half. Out of nowhere, the strangest thing started happening: my clothes dryer, which had always worked *perfectly* up until this point, began shrinking my clothes. First it was my jeans, which I chalked up to the fact that I only wash them a handful of times a year, so they'd probably been ridiculously stretched out. But next it was a skirt, then a few skirts, then every pair of pants and the single pair of shorts I owned. *What the hell?*

I made a note to call the dryer repairman.

Not long after my fortieth birthday, I went for my annual ob-gyn check. I'd been avoiding my scale at home but I knew she was going to make me step on hers—the one humiliatingly positioned right in the hallway where everyone can see you stripping yourself of every last accessory and holding your breath before you step on—so I'd worn a featherlight sundress and my wispiest thong. I kicked off my sandals, took off my clunky watch and stepped onto the scale hesitatingly, terrified to see where the little pointer-thingy would land.

I couldn't believe it. I was the same weight I'd been for as long as I could remember. Exactly. So what the hell was happening?

I brought this mystery up to my very-thin fiftysomething friend Rachel, who gently explained that even when women don't gain weight, everything sort of . . . *shifts* after forty. "I have bulges and pooches all around my middle that I didn't used to have," she insisted.

"At the risk of sounding rude, you are a fucking liar," I told her. "I'm *looking* at you."

"It's not what you can see; it's what you can't see," Rachel insisted.

Apparently, Rachel's secret was something called a Muffin Top Stopper, which is a pretty cute name for a *pants expander*. It seemed you just slipped this thing between the existing button and buttonhole on your jeans, and it bought you two or three extra inches. Never mind that your flabby, fleshy tummy blubber would poke right through the new opening; we're talking full-on muffin-top stopping.

"Please tell me you're kidding," I pleaded.

"I'm not kidding," Rachel insisted. "I know you think I'm so skinny, but honestly, without this thing I'd have flaps of skin hanging over both sides of my jeans."

"I think I'd rather have the flaps," I told her.

I hate the flaps. I really do. And the fleshy skin that oozes out from beneath my bra straps in the back and the new thickness I have in my middle where I am almost positive I used to have a waist (one friend calls it her "meno-pot"). But what am I going to do? Forsake pizza forever? Succumb to the scalpel? Quit my job and never see my kids so I can work out eleven hours a day and then die penniless and estranged from my family but with an extremely toned corpse? What would be the point? Life is hard enough. And besides, bread tastes really, really good. And isn't balance the key to everything?

I know, you probably don't eat bread. Because you read *Wheat Belly*, and you're convinced that carbs are the spawn of

Satan. But life is supposed to be lived—not merely tolerated—and to me, never again enjoying a fresh-baked slice of focaccia or a bowl of French onion soup, which would mostly be broth without that delicious cheese-covered crouton thingy on top, or an occasional bacon cheeseburger *with the bun and everything* doesn't seem worth it.

"But those foods will kill you!" you cry. And you're probably right. But did you ever watch the show *Third Rock from the Sun*? There was this great episode in which the John Lithgow character, Dick—who is a bumbling alien doing a hilariously crappy job of fitting in among his earthling peers—discovers cigarettes. Completely clueless about the fact that smoking is universally considered a vile and reprehensible habit, Dick lights up often and with abandon, chain sucking those sticks down to the barest of butts whenever the urge strikes. His Earthling girlfriend Mary (the brilliant Jane Curtin), of course, is horrified and tries desperately to get him to quit—to no avail.

"But Dick," Mary finally says, appalled, "don't you know that smoking takes years off of your life?"

"Yes!" Dick responds. "But it takes years off the *end* of your life, and those years suck anyway!"

Just something to consider.*

---

* Not the smoking part. You definitely shouldn't smoke. But for the love of garlicky dipping oil, life is short even if you *don't* smoke. Have a fucking piece of bread every once in a while.

CHAPTER 8

At Least I've Got My Health, Mostly

I think I have figured out why people eventually retire, and it's not because we become too old and infirm to get any meaningful work done anymore or because we've stockpiled so much cash that it's no longer necessary to acquire even a single dollar more. No, we give up the careers we've spent a lifetime building because after a certain point, keeping our creaking, aching parts in reasonably working order becomes a full-time job of its own.

It's a little bit shocking, I have to tell you. Up until fairly recently, my annual routine maintenance involved a pap smear and a lecture about the importance of the breast self-exam I was really bad about doing. I didn't even have a regular doctor who didn't specialize in vaginas. If I came down with strep throat or a sinus infection, I went to the closest Urgent Care and waited with all the unwashed masses seven years to see some kid in a white coat claiming to be a medical-school graduate. I vaguely recall having a full physical when I got married and made the very grown-up decision to purchase life insurance—a necessity in the sense that neither my new young husband nor I could afford our mortgage payments solo should *God forbid* something happen to one of us. But beyond that and the occasional teeth cleaning, I had pretty much managed to avoid having any of my orifices probed or my organs prodded on anything resembling a regular basis.

Talk about the good old days. Now it seems my calendar is forever crammed with appointments to see people I have to pay to look at me naked.

" My Welcome-to-Midlife Moment Was . . . "

When I was waiting at the pharmacy for a prescription, and an old guy came up to the counter. The pharmacist asked his birthday, and it wasn't too far from mine.

—KRYSTAL

My dermatologist Rebecca and I are on a first-name basis since my body started producing these random, benign cysts called dermatofibromas.* They're about the size of a big pea or

---

* Even though things ending in *-oma* generally aren't good, if you have to get a cyst, this is the kind I'd recommend.

a small marble and usually pop up on my head—I like to joke that my brain needs more space to house all of its brilliant and witty thoughts—but I've had them removed from my knee and hip, too. While I'm in her exam room, Rebecca likes to put on her magnifying glasses and take her sweet time giving every microscopic inch of my flesh a thorough once-over. This is great fun and not at all humiliating, especially in a frigid, fluorescently lit doctor's office that has a skeleton perched in the corner. ("Not wearing sunscreen can *kill* you," it scolds.) Sometimes Becky takes a few nice close-up pictures of this mole or that freckle, ostensibly for the purpose of baseline comparison, but we all know she probably posts them on Facebook with funny captions, or at least includes them in her medical journal articles. Still, until now everything that's been snipped from my body and sent to the pathology lab (this is standard operating procedure, literally) has been benign, so at least there's that.

Then there's the annual mammogram. I started this enjoyable ritual earlier than most, due to a family history of breast cancer.* And while I am extraordinarily grateful to live in a time and a country where this technology is available to me, every time I see my boob flattened out like a homemade tortilla between icy plates of glass and metal, my singular thought is *Really? This is still the best we've got?* Think about it. We can send monkeys (and humans!) into outer space and sport wear-

---

* I know. You're not supposed to say *cancer* in a funny book. I promise I won't do it again.

able computers with built-in facial recognition software. We can build a working semiautomatic firearm, an acoustic guitar, a glazed ceramic coffee cup, a waterproof bikini, a precise miniature Aston Martin replica, and even human organs with nothing more than a 3-D printer.* We can fuel cars with recycled fryer oil, track the calories we burn with every step we take, and transplant entire faces that have been ravaged by disaster or disease. We've built robotic lifeguards that have pulled people from riptides and saved their lives. You'd think by now we could just swallow a little computer chip that would scan our insides on the way down and transmit all of the data to our doctors' computers in real time before we pooped the thing out. But no. Apparently, figuring out how to get Leonardo DiCaprio to Mars has kept scientists extremely busy.

I actually passed out during a mammogram once. It happened just after a perfect stranger had molested my boob, pulling it up and away from my body and smashing it against one metal plate and holding it there while she lowered another. There I was, all cranked in, when I started to feel funny.

"Is it hot in here?" I asked my molester.

"Not really," she replied, very busy pressing buttons.

"I'm feeling a little dizzy," I told her.

"Do you want me to get you some water?" she asked from very, very far away.

---

* I am not even making that shit up. It scares the crap out of me to think we are beyond anything they could have imagined when they produced *The Jetsons*.

Water? What was water? My body started to break out in an allover sweat. With my one free arm, I tried to wiggle out of my hospital gown. God it was hot. I needed that thing off.

The last thing I remember was hearing my own now-infamous words:

"I'm going down."

I woke up on the floor with my feet up on a chair surrounded by four nurses. They were white as ghosts. One was holding smelling salts underneath my nose. (In case you've never had the pleasure, smelling salts have a unique aroma reminiscent of burnt hair that's been doused in ammonia. If that shit doesn't wake you right up, you're probably dead.) *Where had all of these people come from?* I wondered. *And when?*

"Did I faint?" I asked. I had never fainted in my life.

"You sure did," one of them replied, still looking ashen.

"Does this happen a lot?" I wanted to know. Surely, it must.

"Nope," another said, shaking her head. "Never. Not even once."

I comforted myself with the thought that at least it hadn't happened during a proctology exam.

And then there are the hot flashes. You know how they say "you don't know what you've got until it's gone"? Yeah, they were talking about your fully functioning internal thermostat, the one that told your body to produce copious amounts of sweat only when it was 115 degrees out and/or you were performing an intensely aerobic activity for extended periods of time (not when you were, say, sipping an icy lemonade and flipping through *People* magazine in the air-conditioned hair salon). "Is it hot in here?" you'll ask your husband, your kids, your hairdresser, and the guy in line behind you in Starbucks, and they'll all look at you as if you're on crack. No, it's not hot in there. It's just you. (And you might want to find something to mop your upper lip with before it drips onto your shirt.)

Flattened boobs and overzealous sweat ducts aside, the thing that sidelines me the most these days are the inexplicable bodily injuries. It's not as if I'm out training for triathlons or scaling rock faces or playing roller hockey, so the frequency and severity of these injuries almost always catches me off guard. I work out with some girlfriends, take the occasional barre or Pilates class, and try to thwack at a tennis ball for an hour or so on a quasi-regular basis. I'm in decent enough shape that you'd think I could, for instance, go bowling with my eighty-year-old in-laws without wrenching my back so severely that I'd wind up writhing in bedridden pain for two endlessly long weeks.

You'd be wrong.

In my lifetime I have cracked a few ribs, broken my tailbone, had road rash scoured out of my mangled butt cheek with a scrub brush in the ER, suffered third-degree burns from sticking a bobby pin into an electrical outlet,* and sliced off the tip of my index finger on a mandoline,† and I can still say that throwing out your back is the worst. You really don't know

---

* I was five, okay? It's not like I knew better.

† Fine, I was forty-two that time. I agree, I should have known better. My then six-year-old put it this way: "But why didn't you just use the finger-protector thingy? It's not that complicated."

or appreciate how much you rely on your spine until you tweak it so badly that it hurts to blink and your husband has to carry you to the toilet when you have to use it. *And then wipe you when you're done.* Unfortunately for both of us, whacking out my back is a semiannual occurrence for me.

The last time it happened was during a workout. I was doing a combo squat with an overhead press—using weights, of course—when something snapped. I didn't actually hear it, but man did I feel it. I slowly lowered myself to the ground while my friends watched in horror.

"What's wrong?" Hannah demanded.

"My . . . back . . ." I gasped. "I . . . can't . . . move."

"Oh my gosh, what can we do?" Lety wanted to know.

"There's nothing you *can* do," I whimpered from my yoga mat.

"Can I get you some ice?" Kim asked.

"I think that would be like putting a Band-Aid on a severed limb," I told them. "Seriously, keep going. I'm just going to lie here. You don't get to use me as an excuse not to finish your workout."

"Do you want me to rub it?" Lisa asked.

"Oh God, please don't touch me," I begged.

They continued to offer help, but I insisted I just wanted to lie there and try not to die. After they sweated and stretched, Lisa drove me home. Later, Lety called to apologize.

"We shouldn't have kept working out," she said.

"Why not?" I asked. "I would have. There was nothing you could do."

"Well, when I told my husband what had happened, he said 'I hope you guys moved her out of the way before you finished your workout.' When I told him that *of course we did*, he was like, 'Oh my God, Lety! I was *kidding*! Tell me you didn't keep working out while she was lying on the ground in pain.' So then I felt really bad."

"Honestly," I told her. "If everyone had to stop working out every time I got hurt, you'd all be in really lousy shape."

Here's where things started to get really fun: Because I am completely intolerant of any of the good narcotic-type pain medications—they make me vomit almost immediately, which is not something you want to be doing when your spine is alternately seizing and spasming, and every breath feels like someone is driving an ice pick into it—I had to resort to over-the-counter pain pills. Aside from the hideous "Tylenol Tampering Scare" in the early '80s, a few hundred milligrams of shit I give my kids seemed like a pretty safe, benign choice. I read the ibuprofen directions (something I only do with medication, never when I am, say, assembling a Barbie Dream House or making fettuccine Alfredo) and followed them to the letter, downing two caplets every six hours on the dot. It barely even put a dent in the pain, so I put myself to bed early, praying for the sweet relief of sleep.

I woke up around midnight feeling funny. My face was wet and felt oddly numb. I turned on a light and tapped Joe awake.

"Heysh, Shoe, dosh my fasch look shtrange?" I slurred.

"Jesus Christ, what happened to you?" Joe asked, recoiling in horror.

I stumbled to the bathroom mirror. The right side of my face was hugely swollen and mostly immobile. Clearly, I'd had a stroke. I dimly recalled a FW: FW: FW: email I'd received years ago that covered what to do when someone has a stroke. Were you supposed to check their tongue? Or wrap them in blankets? Was CPR or the Heimlich maneuver involved? *Damn it all to hell, why am I always in such a rush? I should have paid attention to that shit.* But of course I hadn't. Strokes were something old people had. Delete.

After several hours of poking, prodding, peeing, and pricking, the kindly ER doctor calmly presented her diagnosis.

"You've got angioedema," she said.

Didn't *angio* mean heart? Or have something to do with sperm? And wasn't *edema* some sort of swelling? Had I had a sperm-related *heart attack*? I'd just had my cholesterol levels checked, I'll have you know, and I'd been told I had the heart of a twenty-year-old. Plus I hadn't had sex in . . . Jeez, when *was* the last time I'd had sex? I really needed to start making that a priority.

"Angioedema is just a name for tissue swelling," she explained. "It's basically an allergic reaction. In this case, since your blood work ruled out almost everything else, my guess is it was the ibuprofen."

At forty-three, I'd been taking ibuprofen for roughly all of ever. Perhaps not in the horse-killing quantities I'd ingested this time, but still. *I'd followed the directions that were printed right there on the bottle and which you would assume were safety tested for exactly these sorts of purposes.* Did one just up and develop random, potentially fatal allergies after a certain age? Yes, the doctor informed me. Yes, one did.

I was given a prescription for an EpiPen,* which is a giant hotdog-size syringe filled with epinephrine that people with severe, life-threatening allergies must carry at all times,† in case the rapid, sudden swelling that marks an allergic reaction occurs in the airway—which can cause suffocation and death. Should I abruptly feel as if I am being smothered, I am simply to remember instantly where I left my purse last, fish through bags of raisins and grocery receipts and thirty-seven lip glosses to unearth the stupid thing in the bowels of it, gingerly remove the cap, take a deep breath, jam the needle deep into my thigh, and *not panic at all* while I wait for my airway to open itself up again.

Like *that's* going to happen.

(True story: Just this week I was in the bathroom helping my eight-year-old daughter get ready for school when I felt—and then heard—a rumbling. Then it got louder. I assumed it was her older sister upstairs doing one of her famously house-shaking hip-hop dance routines, until that one called from another downstairs room, "Mom, what's *happening*?" Despite exhaustive, repeated training to do exactly the opposite, I screamed "EARTHQUAKE!" at the top of my lungs, grabbed

---

* Naturally, my insurance did not cover the $250 cost, because obviously, they hoped I wouldn't buy it and subsequently die, as I'd become quite a liability of late.

† Apparently I was now one of them. Yippee!

the kid closest to me by the arm and pulled her frantically out the back door. I hadn't "ducked and covered" as I'd been taught to do, and I had *abandoned my husband and first-born child to fend for themselves in a potentially deadly natural disaster.* The quake passed relatively quickly and everyone emerged unscathed if a bit shaky, but I share this story to illustrate the fact that clearly I am not to be trusted to react rationally or intelligently in any life-threatening emergency situation.)

Still, I feel better knowing that EpiPen is almost definitely down there at the bottom of my purse. *[Makes a mental note to check and also update will.]*

" My Welcome-to-Midlife Moment Was . . . "

When I realized I could tell it was going to rain because my knees ached.

—KERRY

In between one or another of the back episodes, I noticed that my shoulder had started making this creaky, popping sound whenever I rotated it. I waited a few weeks, hoping it would go away on its own, but it didn't. In fact, it continued to get even creakier and poppier. Worried it would get to the point where a serious medical intervention would be required, I scheduled an appointment with an orthopedic surgeon.

"What seems to be the problem?" he asked.

"My shoulder is making this awful creaking and popping sound when I rotate it," I told him.

"Let's see," he said, twisting my arm up and around in circles. It popped and creaked beautifully on demand.

"Yup, you've got crepitus," he said, nodding his head.

"Crepitus?" I repeated, terrified. It sounded even worse than angioedema, like decrepit and corpse all rolled into one ugly, damning word. Did I need surgery? Was I going to lose the use of my arm? Or have to have the entire arm amputated? Was it *fatal*?*

"What's . . . *crepitus*?" I finally asked.

"It's when your joints make popping and creaking sounds," the surgeon explained patiently.

"Well, I could have guessed *that*," I said with equal patience. "That's why I'm here. But what *is* it? What causes it? How do you treat it?"

"The sound you hear is bone and cartilage rubbing together," he told me. "It could be a sign of osteoarthritis. Or it could be just age."

I'd known that my body was going to get weaker and saggier and quite possibly shorter and wider throughout this highly amusing maturation process . . . but *louder*?

The doctor didn't recommend surgery, so I employed a strategic and clearly sound approach I came up with that I call *ignoring it completely and continuing about my merry way*. In

---

* In case you hadn't picked up on this fact, I might have a tiny tendency to overreact on occasion, especially where medicine is involved.

time the creepy crepitus packed its bags and found a younger, healthier shoulder to annoy. Or maybe my ears are going, and I just can't hear it anymore.

After the back, shoulder, and angioedema episodes, I woke up one day with a searing pain in my left foot.* Again, I tried to wait it out, and again, it continued to worsen. This time I sought out a foot specialist who diagnosed me with tendonitis and prescribed several weeks in a cast, the result of which was pretty much nothing. I moved on to physical therapy (because I have nothing but time to kill and money to burn!). When that didn't work, I sought a second opinion—which was identical to the first, only this time the prescription was a combination of total immobility plus zero weight bearing, which meant a cast *plus* crutches.

Did you realize that you can't do *anything* when you're on crutches? You can't vacuum, unload the dishwasher, make a stinking bed, or even carry your own cup of coffee. If you don't have a laundry basket on wheels, you're sort of screwed. And you think hot flashes suck on a regular day? Try breaking out in a full-body sweat while you've got two rubber-tipped sticks jammed into your armpits, where they've already rubbed off most of the adjacent skin. *You have to sit down to put on and take off your goddamned underpants.* What's that? Your phone's ringing but you left it outside on the patio and nobody is home to run and get it for you? Man, I hope it wasn't Lottery Head-

---

* And unfortunately, I wasn't able to create amazing paintings with it like Daniel Day-Lewis could in the movie of the same name.

quarters or that hot guy you met last night calling. If you're young and on the fence about having children, the remote possibility that you might one day find yourself needing crutches is argument enough to bite the bullet and get yourself knocked up already. *Because you're going to need help.*

By my second week on crutches, I was getting damned sick of this falling-apart business.

"Maybe you need your chakras cleaned," my friend Tamara suggested.

"I don't know," I said. "Seeing as I've never even had them lightly dusted in my entire life, they're probably disgusting. Are there commercial chakra cleaners out there? Because I'd definitely need the big guns."

"I'm serious," Tamara insisted. "Your chakras are your energy centers, and it sure sounds like you have some stagnating energy."

Of course Tamara is a total whack job (whom I adore because/in spite of this). But the thought that the answer might be as simple as polishing my grubby energy centers was too appealing to resist, so I turned to my guilty-pleasure website, Fiverr.com. Fiverr is the only place I know where you can get, buy, or do just about anything you can think of for exactly five bucks.* It's all kinds of awesome. For a single Lincoln, you can

---

* Unless you care to spring for one of the totally optional extras. Like if you want the guy who jumps around in a chicken suit to make chicken noises or hold up a sign at the same time, you're going to have to pony up a little more. Totally worth it.

get a thousand-word article translated into Mandarin Chinese, have a new logo or business card designed, or hire a hairy guy to sing happy birthday to your mother wearing only a thong and a wooly hat.* I scrolled through the listings, trying to focus—which turned out to be damned near impossible. Celtic cross tarot readings, professional book-cover design, my name written in fruit, my message recorded in "the awesome voice of Sean Connery" . . oooh, that might be fun. Who could I send *that* to? And what should Sean say? Oh crap, what was I here for again? Oh yeah, a professional chakra cleaner. Of course.

After scanning a few offers, I settled on a seller with 100% positive reviews, boasting comments like "felt amazing!" and "my back and knees felt better immediately." The listing said this:

> *When your chakras are spinning properly it leads to good physical and mental health. My job is to clear out any "junk" and get your energy running correctly. I do this either using my pendulum or other energy techniques.*

Awesome, right? I clicked the link, which took me to the PayPal payment page. What's five bucks for spiffy, like-new chakras? Send payment, baby! I then emailed the seller to ask what would happen next. Would we have a phone chat,

---

* *[Adds to cart]*

perhaps? A Skype call? I hoped it wasn't a Skype call. I hate getting out of my bathrobe and putting on clothes if I don't have to, although if it meant happy, well-balanced, sparkly chakras, I suppose I'd do it.

After three days of nothing, I got this message from my personal chakra-doctor:

> Hi there!
>
> I checked your chakras, and the only thing I noticed was the heart chakra was a little darker overall. It could be your color, but usually I see an emerald green and yours was darker overall. I cleared it out a little. You're going to have to do the rest.
>
> My take on that is there is some stress, known or unknown, that is affecting you. It could be from work or home. Meditation and grounding will help tremendously.
>
> Anyhow, I cleaned out and fluffed up all the other chakras, and they are rotating correctly.
>
> Let me know of any changes.

Really? That was it? Without knowing a single thing about me—including where I live, which you'd think she/he would need to know in order to actually *find* my grimy little chakras— a stranger of undetermined gender and training was able to access my energy centers and then (you got this part, right?)

fluff them up? I know, I'm a sucker. A sucker out five whole bucks, which could have bought me a venti triple-shot latte or my name written on someone's size six feet. Next time, I'll know which is the better investment.

I guess with age comes wisdom.

CHAPTER 9

It's Just a Car
(Except That It's Not)

My husband, Joe, and I have never, ever agreed on the proper way to own cars. My belief—which technically was my dad's, but you pretty much need a stick of dynamite or a serious brain injury to erase the shit that gets drilled into your head when you're a kid—is that you buy a two-year-old car, drive it for two years, and then sell it and repeat. This way, you never pay that initial depreciation (which my dad referred to as "the ass-hole tax you shell out for the privilege of driving a brand-new car off the lot the first time"), and you never really get into any major repairs. You're sort of *borrowing* the car, and you maintain it meticulously, keeping painstaking records of your diligent efforts, before handing it off to the next poor sucker who will probably run it into the ground, because nobody takes care of their cars as well as you do.

Joe's car philosophy is pretty much the diametrical opposite. "I'm not buying somebody else's headache," he grumbles as he's forking over the asshole tax. Oh yes, he buys brand-new cars, gets the oil changed every five minutes, buys seat covers to protect the upholstery,* has them professionally detailed on a regular basis—none of that $14 car wash business for my husband—and drives them until they die. I'll point out here that the man has been driving for thirty-four years and he is on his *third car.* (For comparative purposes: I've been driving for twenty-two years—if you don't count the years I lived carless in New York City—and am on my eleventh.)

So it's a major headline-making coup that he has finally agreed that it's time to upgrade my twelve-year-old model,† one that runs perfectly well (although is far from pristine, thanks kids!) and hasn't given us a moment's trouble.

"What about a Ford?" Joe suggested straightaway.

"Too masculine," I replied.

"Jeep?" he said.

"Too utilitarian," I insisted.

"You do know what that word means, right?" he countered.

I ignored him.

---

* This is a great investment if you want your seats to look perfect when you eventually have the thing towed to a junkyard.

† Read: *has gotten so beaten down by me bitching about it that he's willing to spend tens of thousands of dollars to make it stop.*

"How about an Acura?" Joe suggested.

"Too bubbly," I told him.

"Too *bubbly*?" he asked. "What the hell does that mean?"

"Look at them," I responded.

"Good luck with your car hunt, honey," Joe said.

We went back and forth on the third-row seat option—me insisting we needed it because as our kids get older they are both going to want to bring friends everywhere we go, and Joe maintaining that if we didn't have the extra room, then we'd have a built-in, airtight argument for forced family bonding.

"What about field trips? They never have enough drivers for those, and if we had a third row, we could take six kids," I argued.

"So I'm going to drop forty thousand bucks because all of the other parents suck and refuse to drive on these hellish expeditions?" Joe barked. "You're going to have to do better than that, Jenna."

I was just a few weeks into the search when I heard a purry, gravelly voice on the radio telling me about a *sexy new car* and something I didn't really hear about gas mileage. The commercial was for some new energy/hybrid model that I am pretty sure you can drive to Australia and back on a single tank of gas. But the record-breaking fuel efficiency wasn't the big sell here; the husky-voiced, faceless spokesmodel (who I am convinced was actually *Modern Family*'s Julie Bowen even though she said something like: "Hi, I'm Elizabeth Smith . . .") spent the better portion of her allotted air time raving about how this car was some sort of sex machine on wheels, possibly hotter than Fifty Shades of Anything on Earth. I was picturing an Alfa Romeo or maybe a Porsche Cayenne and getting a little wound up just thinking about it.

I actually pulled over to Google this vehicular Channing Tatum, it sounded *that* amazing. Talk about a bait and switch. I mean, the wonder car in question wasn't hideous or anything—it basically looked like any other egg-shaped four-door mom car on the road—but calling it *sexy* would be like calling Kim Kardashian a gifted actress or rice cakes a delectable snack: a ~~wee bit of a~~ gigantic stretch.

I want a sexy car. I do. Not necessarily vintage-Mustang sexy or even Mini Cooper Convertible sexy, although those would be dreamy. It doesn't even have to be brand-new sexy. But made-in-this-decade-and-doesn't-smell-like-rotten-milk sexy would be nice. I want a car I'm proud to get into in the Trader Joe's parking lot and one I'm not ashamed to valet park at the occasional fancy restaurant. I want a car that has at least a few bells and whistles that make the biweekly schlep to Costco slightly less torturous.* I want a car that has a voice inside the dashboard to tell me where to turn, preferably with an English accent and an excess of patience. I want a car with DVD players—two of them with wireless headphones, please!—in the headrests, so that my husband doesn't have to bungee our portable model ghetto-style between the front seats, and so that we don't have to listen to the shoot-me-now

---

* Electric windows and a tape deck no longer count as "bells and whistles," dear.

Pippi Longstocking theme song every single time we drive to LAX. I want a car whose "check engine" light isn't permanently illuminated and whose seatback pockets don't have liquefied Red Hots ground into their corners. Oh, and I'd really like a car that has one of those nifty backup cameras so that I wouldn't reverse right over my friend Barb's trashcan—again—and drag it several hundred yards down her street while all the neighbors run out of their houses to see what the commotion is.

(Aside: Just last night I mentioned to Joe how cool it would be to have just such a backup camera. His response: "Honey, you'd *still* back into shit, and then we'd have to pay to get the camera fixed, so really that feature is a liability, not an asset." The worst part is, he's probably right.)

My girlfriends have been snapping up fun, sexy cars left and right lately, and it's hard not to be noticeably jealous. Kelly got herself a badass Corvette that she uses to tool around town just for kicks (she's also got an SUV for her many kid duties). Having two cars is a luxury I can only dream of. Tristan, a petite, drop-dead gorgeous, real-life cowgirl, traded in her station wagon for one of those gigantic trucks with wheels the size of Texas so she can haul her horse trailer into the backcountry on a whim. (And if you think a chick in a pickup isn't hot, I can give you the names of a dozen local doctors who specialize in whiplash who will set you straight.) When Vicky's oldest went off to college, leaving her with a mere three children to shuttle to their sundry activities, she downsized from a well-worn Suburban that could carry an entire soccer team to a zippy new Mercedes two-door. You want to talk about bells and whistles?

You can get a professional-strength *back massage* right in the passenger seat while Vicky drives you to Starbucks. When the economy took a crap and finances got a little tighter for Michelle, the poor girl was forced to trade in her luxurious Lexus . . . for a brand-new Cadillac. ("It doesn't even have a GPS!" she insisted when I mocked her "downgrade.") Me, I'm happy when the windshield wipers on my milk-mobile move enough dirt away for me to be able to see the road.

Sometimes I think I'm nuts to have such option envy. A car, after all, is merely a vehicle of transport, a means of getting you from point A to point B without having to hoof it, hitch-hike, or (by far the worst) catch the local uptown bus. Have we all gotten so completely spoiled filthy rotten that we need vehicles that feature foot-operated liftgates (BMW, Mercedes, Ford), automatic seat-temperature controls (Lexus), refrigerators built right into the consoles (Ford), and back-up collision intervention systems that actually apply the brakes *for you* if you're about to hit something (Cadillac, Infinity)?*

Apparently, we have. The whole thing is ludicrous and excessive, and let me apologize in advance for what I am going to say next, but *I want a piece of that action.*

I've had some pretty sweet cars in my lifetime—at least the part of my lifetime that didn't also involve lice combs and rectal thermometers. I was driving a cute little Saab convertible

---

* Seriously! How awesome is *that*?

when I got pregnant with my first child. Pretty much as soon as my pee dried on that stick and I realized I was incubating an actual person, I put up the top and stuck a FOR SALE sign in the back window. A sporty convertible just wasn't safe enough for my unborn child—or for somebody who was about to become someone else's *mother*, for that matter. I never for a nanosecond considered getting a minivan—it's not in my nature—but I did trade my fun, sexy ride for the biggest, boxiest SUV I could find and also afford. It looked exactly like all of the other cars in the Kindermusik parking lot, so I was pretty sure I'd made the right choice.

My tank of a glorified truck has served me well. It's carted countless kids on incalculable field trips and hauled at least four billion rolls of toilet paper and three hundred bottles of ketchup home from various big-box stores. It's gotten my family safely to and from Sea World and Disney, ski trips and camping excursions, family gatherings and funerals. The doors are scratched, the mats are trashed, and there are faint green stains on both of the backseat headrests from the temporary dye we put in the kids' hair every year on School Spirit Day. For some inexplicable reason, the roof's interior looks as if it's been danced on by an army of Irish cloggers fond of jumping in mud puddles. I'll bet if you bothered to look under the backseats—which I wouldn't advise—you'd find an ocean of goldfish crackers, several thousand lollipop wrappers, a dozen or more mangled water bottles, and enough crayons to outfit a craft-loving miniature army.

My friend Starshine,* a wise woman and brilliant writer, has a very pragmatic car approach that I wish like hell I could adopt. In a column she penned about her decision not to fix a dent she suffered after a fender-bender in her then newish car, Starshine wrote:

> *To me, a car isn't something to be protected; it's there to protect me and anyone else brave enough to ride with me . . . It's a stick-shift suit of armor, a highway-rated hazmat suit, if you will. The exterior is scraped, dented, and, um, impaled so that I am not. No one blubbers when an umbrella gets wet, or a helmet gets dinged, right? If a car is damaged and its passengers intact, it means the thing is* working.

If these are the criteria by which we are judging, then my car works. It gets me where I'm going and protects me from the elements and puts a critical shield between me and the very large trucks on the highway. It almost always starts and has never been in a major accident. (The trash can incident doesn't count. And neither does the time that I drove away from the gas station pump with the hose *still in my gas tank*, because no people or cars were hurt in either instance even though the pump one was probably caught on surveillance camera and I could be arrested for destruction of property and possibly larceny at any minute because I didn't actually stop or go back;

---

* Yes, that is her real name. Starshine Roshell; Google her. And then subscribe to her newsletter and buy her books because she is wickedly funny.

eventually the hose fell out.) While in all of these senses my battered SUV is doing its job, if cars were pickup lines, mine would whimper, "Hi, I'm a little run-down and in desperate need of a shower, but you can probably depend on me." Not exactly the precursor to "take me home or lose me forever."

But dependability is huge. Because who has time for a breakdown, vehicular or otherwise? Not me. I barely have time to get this kid to gymnastics and that one to volleyball and run to the farmer's market and the dry cleaner and the drugstore before I sweep back to grab them both and rush them home—rattling off a list of the things I expect them to do the nanosecond we walk in the door—and get something resembling dinner on the table as it is. I need to know with 100 percent certainty that my car is going to start up when I have exactly six minutes to get where I need to be.* A new car, I explained to Joe, wasn't about Bluetooth connection or MP3 players or satellite radio;† it was about peace of mind.

"Happy wife, happy life," he sighed.

So we have been looking. During this car hunt, I have come to understand deeply that cars say something about their owners, whether we want to admit it or not. They don't always say flattering things, of course. Nobody looks at the hot college coed getting into her souped-up muscle car and thinks, *I'll bet*

---

* Yes, I know there's no such thing as 100 percent certainty, but damn it I want my car to come close.

† Okay fine, it was about those things, too.

she's a really nice girl who volunteers at the retirement home downtown and can knit a lovely afghan. Am I right? The slick-haired grandpa cruising the main drag in his Porsche convertible obviously is attention starved and on the prowl for some starry-eyed arm candy; the down-on-his-luck Realtor who pulls his brand-new Range Rover up to the rat-infested rental apartment he shares with four roommates clearly is high on a dangerous cocktail of insecurity and hopeful optimism.

The funny thing is, in every other area of my life I truly don't care what people think about me. (You can't write books and talk about your vagina in graphic detail if you do, trust me.) Sure, I love having great friends and I try to be a nice person, but it's not like I give a shit if you think I'm too old to wear thigh-high boots with skinny jeans or you disapprove of the fact that I reward my kids with cash for every perfect score they get on a test. But the day I test drove one of those über-posh luxury cars that gets single-digit gas mileage, even though I loved every luxurious inch of it and maybe even had been staring at a picture of one on my Vision Board for several years,* my very first thought was I might as well order the ASS*HOLE vanity plate and SCREW MOTHER EARTH THIS CAR'S THE SHIT AND YOU'RE JUST JEALOUS bumper sticker now. Even if I could have afforded it—which would have necessitated selling my shriveled-up eggs, becoming a surrogate, or getting a weekend pole-dancing job, none of which seemed entirely

---

* Don't judge me. It can't hurt.

prohibitive if it weren't for the MPG—I just couldn't do it. I couldn't be that guy.

So I'm still looking. And I'm confident that any day now I am going to find a sexy, sturdy, environmentally friendly transportation machine that has enough gadgetry to make me giddy and a price tag that doesn't make my husband choke. What? It could happen.

CHAPTER 10

You Can Trim Your Own Damned Nose Hairs

When Joe and I were dating, I spent hours—sometimes days—preparing for every encounter. I'd try on a dozen or more outfits before deciding on the perfect combination of stylish yet casual, sultry but not slutty. I'd take long, luxurious baths, lathering up with scented oils and shaving every inch of my body that I had deemed should be hairless with surgical precision. If I'd had time, I might have shopped for a new bra and panty set. After tidying up my apartment and making sure my nails were painted and my roots were sun-kissed perfection, I'd brush and floss and style and straighten and stock my purse with an assortment of breath mints. I wanted to delight and impress Joe, enchant and enrapture him, and no effort or inconvenience was too great. Sometimes it's hard to believe that all of that was for the same guy I now have full-on, in-person conversations with while I am pooping.

You hear a lot about the importance of "maintaining romance" in long-term relationships, but I'm not really sure how to do it. If you've managed to sustain an ounce of mystery about yourself after thousands of days of living with the same person, you've figured out something that I very clearly haven't.

I can prove it. On a date night recently, Joe leaned across the table, took both of my hands in his, and whispered to me in a husky voice, "Tell me something about you that I don't know."

Totally fucking romantic, right? *I know.* I thought so, too. Then I sat there looking like I'd just had my pupils dilated for several minutes or been asked to name the U.S. presidents in order, dizzy with the realization that I couldn't think of a single semi-interesting thing about me that my husband didn't already know.

"Have I told you about the time Pam and I met those guys, and the one guy asked her to—"

"Lick his stomach," Joe finished my sentence. "Yeah, I've heard that one."

"How about the night I went to that big boxing match with my dad—"

"And you fell off the stage, chair and all, and everyone in the entire place was staring and pointing and laughing at you?" Joe said.

"Well, did you know that when I was a little kid, I thought I was going to become a teacher?" I asked.

"Because you thought you had to," Joe explained for me. "And you thought that the kids who were going to be doctors were at the hospital wearing tiny scrubs and learning about medicine, and the kids who were going to be farmers were out in the fields in big hats, or something like that."

I slumped in my chair.

"I hate green peppers," I told him. "Like, I *really* hate them."

"I know," he said. "And cantaloupe and black pepper and hard-boiled eggs and scary movies and walking on the right side of anyone."

I slumped down even farther.

"At least I listen to you," he said, picking up on my despair.

Of course it isn't a bad thing that my husband knows me so well. I mean, that's what marriage is all about, the blending of lives and the merging of souls and the completing-each-other shit you see in movies. It's sweet and even romantic, in a weird way. But are we doomed because we have no mystery, no excitement? Why hadn't I thought to save a sliver of secrecy, a nugget of intrigue, something that I could whip out a few decades later—when we'd been looking at each other's faces for so long we almost forgot what they looked like—to spice things up? The man I once would have scaled a treacherous rock wall to spend a romantic evening with had seen me floss my teeth, change my tampon, dye my gray roots, struggle into pantyhose, pluck my eyebrows, pick my zits, don a nose strip and eye mask and ear plugs to sleep, and give birth to two nine-pound babies—once without a working epidural. I thought about that scene in *Fried Green Tomatoes* where the (impossibly young, in retrospect) Kathy Bates character attends a "put the spark back into your marriage" seminar and tries wrapping herself in six miles of cellophane as a sexy surprise for her husband (who crushes her by accusing her of going insane, which is totally what my husband would do—right before he ripped the cellophane off with his teeth). Somehow I don't think a Saran Wrap dress could undo countless years of waking up next to the same someone's hideous morning breath or mopping up their vomit every time they get the stomach flu or go a little overboard at the office holiday party.

" My Welcome-to-Midlife Moment Was . . . "

When I was telling my husband a story about this middle-aged woman, and he stopped me cold by saying, "Hon, you are a middle-aged woman." Ugh.

—JODI

It's a blessing and a curse, being in this place of comfortable marital security. On one hand, you've got someone who will come right out and tell you if you have broccoli in your teeth or if you neglected to apply enough deodorant, somebody who will lie to you and tell you that you don't need a face-lift and that he *can* see the triceps muscles you've been working diligently to unearth, somebody who's seen you naked on numerous occasions without laughing or cringing or running screaming into the next room. On the other hand, you also have evenings out that look like this:

. . . .

[Sitting at a stoplight on the way to dinner.]

ME: What are you *doing*?

JOE: I'm trying to *[yank]* pull out *[tug]* this three-inch *[rip]* nose hair. Where did it come from, anyway? Damn it, I can't get it. Hey, your fingers are smaller, and you have nails. Can you grab it?

ME: You want me to pull your nose hair out?

JOE: Well, I can't sit there at dinner with it just hanging out like this. You didn't notice it before we left?

ME: I was very busy trying to squeeze into these Spanx, thank you very much. I think I have manicure scissors in the glove box. *[Finds scissors, hands them to Joe. The light turns green.]*

JOE: Hold the wheel while I do this.

ME: I don't think this is such a great idea.

[Joe sticking scissors tips up his nose and snipping randomly; Jenna gripping steering wheel with white knuckles.]

JOE: Shit, I can't see it without my cheaters. You do it.

ME: *Honey, I would rather not stick scissors up your nose while you're driving. I'll do it when we get to the restaurant.*

And, of course, I did, because it turned out Joe forgot his reading glasses* (which always makes for a fun and romantic

---

* For some odd reason, unlike nearly every one of my friends, I don't need these yet. I feel like the lone eighth-grade girl who hasn't gotten her period over here. *And now I'm certain that between the writing and publishing of this book I'll be wearing 2.0s at least, because of karma.*

game of "Wait, Read Me the Entrée Specials Again" at restaurants) so he simply couldn't.

"You're going to write about this," Joe accused me as I stashed my manicure scissors back in the glove box.

"Are you kidding me?" I asked, offended. "Of *course* I'm going to write about this! This shit is comedy gold right here."

Like I said, the man knows me inside and out.

After we ate—an activity my husband is famous for doing with incomparable thoroughness—our server came to clear our plates.

"Yeah, I hated it," Joe told the guy, gesturing at his practically licked-clean dish.

"Hahahahaha," I trilled on cue.

"I can see that," our server said knowingly, whisking away the spotless evidence.

I'm going to guess that in our seventeen years together, Joe and I have eaten an average of at least one meal out a week—plus at least one or two weeks a year when we are on vacation and we get to enjoy twenty-one restaurant meals. Using this rough calculation, I have heard my husband utter *that exact line* approximately one thousand four hundred times. If I didn't madly love the man, or I had years of bitter resentment born of unmet needs and unheard desires festering in me, I can see where this might make me want to stick something sharp into his eye socket and twist it around a few dozen times for good measure. But I do and I don't, respectively, so his attempted joke is actually endearing. It's one of his *things* that I'd miss tragically if it went away. It would be that "Yeah, I hated it" line—not his dashing good looks or prowess with power tools or skills on the basketball court or anything else the rest of the world can plainly see—that I'd get most choked up on if I were delivering his eulogy today.

There was a breakthrough, pivotal scene in the epically good movie *Good Will Hunting*, where Robin Williams plays a therapist reminiscing about his dead wife with his patient (Matt Damon). "She used to fart in her sleep," Williams tells the clueless Damon character during an otherwise unproductive therapy session. "One night it was so loud it woke the dog up . . . She's been dead two years, and that's the shit I remember . . . little things like that, those are the things I miss the most. Those little idiosyncrasies that only I knew about; that's what made her my wife. People call these things imperfections, but they're not. No, that's the good stuff."

That.

I've studied and written about relationships long enough to know that the first blush of new love—that heady, lustful, who-cares-if-we-sleep-we'll-sleep-when-we're-dead phase— ultimately and invariably morphs into what experts call "deep feelings of attachment."* It's the normal cycle of things, this progression from childish infatuation to real, mature love. It's what separates teenagers from adults and one-night stands from life partners. And frankly, it would be next to impossible

---

* And nothing says "I have deep feelings of attachment for you" like having a full-on, in-person conversation with someone while you are pooping . . . am I right?

to raise children and run a household and not lose our jobs if we were still ripping each other's clothes off at the end of every meal or sometimes in the middle of it.*

"I feel really lucky," my friend Wendy says when talking about her husband, Todd. "Think about the things that attract you to someone when you're dating. You're not necessarily out there looking for a man who will be able to comfort you when your cat dies or who will be a firm-but-loving disciplinarian when you have kids. You want a fun guy, a guy who'll take you out dancing all night and blow his rent money whisking you off on a romantic weekend getaway. You want a guy who will make you laugh and maybe one who is a little bit dangerous and even slightly damaged, because you want to be the one to tame him or fix him or change him or whatever it is you think he needs. But in reality, those aren't necessarily the things that make for a solid lifetime partner."

I feel pretty fucking lucky, too, I have to tell you. I never could have imagined, when I was in my twenties and dating this handsome, floppy-haired, briefcase-carrying kayak guide I'd become utterly smitten with and wanted more than anything in the world to make fall in love with me, that one day I would call him at work and ask him to pick up some hemorrhoid cream for me on his way home. I couldn't have pictured standing naked in front of him in my aunt and uncle's guest bedroom while he used his T-shirt to stop the menstrual blood

---

* Although my husband insists that it could be done and frequently begs for the opportunity to try.

that was pouring down my leg from hitting our gracious hosts' beautiful, seafoam green carpet. I would have punched you in the face for suggesting that one day Joe and I might occasionally find ourselves playing Dutch Oven in bed or that I'd agree to give him a blowjob in exchange for the pleasure of popping a pimple on his back.* I might have fainted from the humiliation of the mere suggestion that one day, when I was recovering from a tendon injury, that I'd let this still-hot Adonis watch my naked middle-aged ass hobble away from the bed on crutches, wearing nothing but a boot cast and a watch. And never in my wildest fantasies would I have believed that I would allow this hunky man of my fantasies into a fluorescently lit fitting room with me to help me decide if the tankini I'm considering does or doesn't do a good enough job of covering my stretch marks.

Even if you saw your own parents get to this midlife marriage place, there's a good chance that now that you're in it, it's not exactly what you thought it would be like. When you get married—even if your husband looks exactly like his father so you have a pretty good idea where *that's* going—you just don't picture yourselves ten or thirty years older, sprawled on your faded, cat-scratched couch watching *The Bachelor* in matching earphones and glasses. Oh, you might *try* to picture your future selves, but in the image you conjure, the couch is spiffy and new, and you're both still spry and fit and hopelessly in love. If you

---

* He thinks I'm disgusting, too, but honestly, I cannot keep my hands off a perfectly ripe zit.

even bothered to consider that pesky "till death do us part" clause in your marriage contract (which you may not have, seeing as you were a bit light-headed from starving yourself so that you could be your lifetime skinniest on your wedding day), you surely didn't pause to wonder what it looked like to slowly grow old next to somebody else who is doing the exact same thing.

Some people take one look at that shit, and they freak out and bolt. It's happened to a bunch of my friends—they ask their husbands to pass the milk at breakfast, and the husbands pour some on their cereal and hand over the carton before casually announcing that they "just aren't in love" anymore and want a divorce. The guys almost always go out and immediately find a young, hopelessly dumb trophy girlfriend, diddle around with that for a year or two before realizing they have nothing at all in common with this new, nubile partner besides being hopelessly dumb and come crawling back, begging for their old wives and lives back. That conversation usually looks a lot like this:

HIM: You were the best thing I ever had, and I blew it. I totally blew it. I threw it all away—you, our future, our family . . .

HER: You sure did.

HIM: Please take me back. I'll do whatever it takes, anything you want. Anything at all. Just say the word and I'll do it.

HER: Hmmm . . . Will you die a slow, painful death so that I can collect a fat life-insurance check? Actually, make that a fast, painful death. I could use a vacation.

HIM: How about I'll go to therapy and buy you a Mercedes and get in really great shape and bring you flowers every single week and take an ad out in the *New York Times* telling the world that I'm a total asswipe?

HER: *I'd prefer the check.*

When this very scenario happened to one our closest couple friends, like everyone else we knew I put the guy—I'll call him Rat Bastard—at the tippy top of my shit list. Then I did my very best to avoid him because I was genuinely afraid I might accidentally smile at him or kick him in the nut sack. I wasn't sure which would be worse.

"You know," my annoyingly wise husband pointed out, "Rat Bastard did what we've always said we would do if we wanted out. He didn't go have some ridiculous affair with a teenage underwear model, and he didn't try to slowly annoy her to death so that she'd be forced to leave *him*. He realized that he was unhappy, and he admitted it. Why do you hate him so much for that?"

"Because he didn't even fucking *try* to fix it, that's why," I screamed, because I'm a screamer when I'm worked up or pissed off. "Ooh, I'm just not *super-happy*," I added in a mock-baby voice. "Big fucking deal! Life is hard. *Marriage* is hard. He made a commitment—for better or for worse—and he has a family and a wife who sacrificed her career for his, and then all of a sudden it's not all kittens and sunshine, so he just up and *leaves*? What a luxury that would be! 'Maybe there's something better out there. Why don't I go check it out and see? If not, I'll be right back.' It's just lame. It's weak and stupid and immature and selfish and lame."

"Remind me never to leave you," Joe said.

"I wouldn't if I were you," I told him. "If you think I'm a bitch to be married to, just wait until we're divorced."

I was reading just this week about a new kind of prenuptial agreement that alternately intrigued and confused me. Remember the friendly, old-fashioned "what's mine stays mine if we ever split up so screw you if you think you're going to bleed me dry someday, you gold-digging bitch" contract? Yeah, that's obsolete. Today's couples are drawing up legally vetted lists of marital demands and outlining the very specific and often costly penalties their partners will incur for not meeting them. By signing these agreements, young and in-love couples are predetermining—*for the rest of ever*, mind you—how often they'll have sex, how they'll spend their free time, what they are and aren't allowed to do and wear, and what exactly counts as "cheating" (same-sex third base, allowed for her if he can watch; opposite-sex first base, punishable to maximum extent for both, etc). Specific stipulations the article highlighted that various couples have outlined in their new-fashioned prenups include:

- The wife isn't allowed to play the piano when the husband is home.
- The husband has to pay the wife $50,000 each time he impregnates her.
- Every time the husband is rude to the wife's parents, he forks over ten grand.

- The wife can't wear anything green.
- The husband gets $100,000 if his wife's weight tops 170 pounds.*
- The wife isn't allowed to cut her hair.†
- If the husband cheats, he must pay his wife up to $5 million.‡

A marriage counselor quoted in the article urged couples to try to get their intended to agree to sex at least once or twice a week, adding "it's nice to have a contract and say, look, we did agree to this."

Yeah, wouldn't it be nice if you had a promissory sex schedule written by your newlywed self twenty or thirty years later? Um, at the risk of offending any overly optimistic newlyweds out there, NO, IT FUCKING WOULD NOT. It would suck complete and total ass.

If you've been married for even half a decade, think back to your engagement days for a second. *Of course you would have agreed to a biweekly shag!* Back then you were fit and energetic and overtaken by hormones, and you could do it five times in a single night! Twice a week was for pussies, for crying out loud. You might even have been too insulted to sign such a thing. It's

---

* I hope she has a pregnancy counter-clause. I'm just saying.

† One can only pray that he means "into a different hairstyle" and not "ever," because that would just get nasty.

‡ Seems fair.

worth pointing out that back then you probably didn't have nine kids needing their asses wiped before begging for "one more book" or aging, crotchety parents living in your house with you or the stress of making your next mortgage payment, and you honestly couldn't fathom being so exhausted that you'd pick twenty extra minutes of sleep over food, sex, shopping, a massage, or anything on TV. *I'll have sex with you all day every day, multiple times, in any room and in any position and with any props your little heart desires, you big stud muffin,* you would have promised, in writing, before a notary public if it was required or requested. And you would have wholeheartedly meant it and believed you were good for it, too. Nobody could call you a liar; you just didn't know what you didn't know.

One has to wonder: What do these couples do when, twenty-five years from now, she gets fed up with dragging thirteen feet of split ends behind her and chops that shit off, or he has an affair with his slutty secretary but can't fork over five million cool ones like he swore in writing he would? What if he has gallbladder surgery or testicular torsion and can't get it up for a while, effectively denying his wife the four-to-ten shags per month that he promised her would be available to her for the duration of their union? What if his mother buys her a nasty-ass emerald sweater for Christmas and begs her to put it on, right then and there, for a family photo? Is she supposed to refuse her mother-in-law this simple, harmless indulgence because she promised she'd never wear green?

It's all absurd, and not just because, at least in the article in question, the lists seem to be heavily skewed in the husbands' favor. It's absurd because marriage is as dynamic as the two people in it. And like the two people in it, if it's not changing and growing, it dies. Plans and priorities and bodies change; obstacles crop up; hairstyles go in and out of vogue; sometimes tragedy strikes. "The best-laid schemes of mice and men," poet Robert Burns famously wrote, "often go awry." Or as I like to say, shit happens—shit that you never saw coming and didn't have the wits or the wherewithal to prepare for in that other faraway lifetime.

Part of what keeps my own marriage going, beyond the fact that I really enjoy having someone to run to the store for hemorrhoid cream for me, is that we are who we are *because* we agreed to spend the entirety of our lives together and because of every experience we've shared. We've been through a lot, Joe and I. We've traveled the world, brought new people into existence, bought and sold homes and cars and big-ticket furniture items, buried pets and parents together. We've nursed each other's wounds, forgiven each other a thousand transgressions, and survived earthquakes and wildfires and terrifying, turbulent, transoceanic flights. We've assembled dozens of children's toys and accessories—and I'm talking monstrosities with a million different parts, including a play house, a boat-shaped sandbox, and a four-piece wooden kitchen set—without killing each other. We may weigh a tiny bit more than we did when we got married and have sex a little less,* but despite the

---

* Or a lot.

nose hair incident and countless others like it, I am still wildly attracted to my husband. I love him more wholly and more profoundly than I did the day I promised I'd be true to him until one of us would be given the heart-wrenching task of scattering the other's ashes. I respect him more, too, because I've seen him handle flat tires and disasters involving sewage and demanding kids with humor and grace. I may be slightly less painstaking in my grooming and date prep these days, and he may be somewhat less patient and attentive, but we both know we're lucky. And I'm really glad his are the only nostrils I will be asked to tidy until one of us dies.

CHAPTER 11

····················

Screw the Rainy Day:
I Just Want Enough Money
to Pay for My Funeral

Karen Carpenter tragically taught us that you most definitely can be too thin, but I've yet to find living (or dead) proof that you can be too rich. In fact, while economists used to claim that increasing income did little to boost well-being, new research suggests that, on average, the more money you have, the happier you are.

I know. No shit, right?

Not that we can't all list at least a handful of miserable, disgustingly well-to-do SOBs we know. But I'm pretty sure the researchers are talking about generally likeable people here, ones who work their asses off or maybe even win the lottery or land a sweet inheritance but still remain likeable even when they're flying their private jets to the Caribbean or lounging on their ninety-foot yachts. For those people, the ones like you and I will be when the gods of fortune finally decide to answer our prayers, more bank equals more bliss.

While I would consider myself almost obnoxiously happy, I am definitely not rich. (So can you imagine how repulsively *ecstatic* I would be if I got a financial windfall? Honestly, it boggles the mind.) I'm far from poor, of course, especially relative to a homeless guy living under an overpass or a commission-only door-to-door encyclopedia salesman. But as I creep ever closer to what some people refer to as "retirement age," I'm feeling some serious financial anxiety. After all, if I want to stop working, say, *ever*, I'm going to need some cash in reserves. And how exactly is one supposed to stockpile a respectable amount of money to live on while also saving for weddings and college tuitions and vacations and home improvements and the drive-through, incision-less full face- and body lift they are going to invent any day now?

Experts say ours is the first generation who will fail to live better than our parents did. While our moms and pops socked away an average of 10 percent of their incomes every month, most of us don't even save a measly 5 percent. Our folks managed it, of course, because they didn't have to pay for everyone in the house to have unlimited texting on their fancy new smartphones and enjoy nine hundred premium cable channels plus Netflix every month. They didn't sign us up for private voice lessons and pricey tennis clinics and posh sleepaway camps; they told us to "go outside and find a stick to play with," and holy hell would rain down if we didn't get our asses home before those damned streetlights came on. They didn't stock our forty-dollar Pottery Barn lunch boxes with pre-packaged, organic, gluten-free delights that cost nine dollars a pop; you got a bruised apple and a PB&J on Wonder Bread in a paper bag (seventeen cents, max) and you were grateful for it.*

My problem—and possibly yours—is that I like stuff. I like sparkly baubles and really soft blankets and useful gadgets and pretty much anything pink. I adore Depression glass and Egyptian cotton sheets and hobnail serving bowls, and you might want to get out of my way in any candle aisle. Unfortunately, nice things are everywhere we turn, and we can have all of them if we're willing to go to the great effort of swiping a piece of plastic through a machine and signing the little electronic screen.

Of course sometimes when we throw caution to the wind and buy something especially nice, we are afraid to actually *use* it,† seeing as we might ruin or break or lose it in the process, and then we'd be right back where we started, except minus the money we paid for the awesome thing and with the sad, ironic knowledge of how awesome it was to have had it at all.

In my house we have a thing about knives. Joe and I like to cook,‡ and we like to eat, so we spend probably more money

---

* Uphill in the snow both ways, damn it.

† By "we" I clearly mean "our husbands."

‡ Okay, we don't *always* like to cook, but we enjoy good food, and we're not trust-funders, which means we can't eat out twenty-one meals a week or hire a private, live-in chef.

than we should on kitchen contraptions. We have damned near every chef's tool ever invented (see the bit above about being cosmically powerless to resist nice stuff), but man do we love our knives.

True story: When we got married those many years ago, we registered for knives. Not a set of them, mind you. We picked out our dream cutlery collection, each individual knife at a time—because the one occasion in your life when other people are shelling out for you to have a few top-of-the-line gadgets is no time to scrimp, right? Anyway, when my mom asked which item on our registry I wanted most, I salivated as I described the specific high-carbon, precision-forged chef's knife of my dreams.

"That knife costs a hundred and seventy-five dollars," my mom said, staring openmouthed at my registry printout.

"I know," I told her. "It's a really great knife."

"But you can get a whole knife block for that much money," she insisted.

"I don't want fifteen decent knives," I tried to explain. "I want one amazing one."

My mom, who'd been raised by extremely frugal Depression-era parents, literally couldn't do it—she couldn't buy a single mind-blowing knife knowing that she could give us a shit-ton of mediocre knives for the same price. So she sent me a gift card to the store, and I bought the knife myself. Joe and I use that knife daily, fight over it frequently, and never once have I regretted opting for quality over quantity.

With that in mind, I recently bought ~~us~~ Joe a new set of steak knives ~~because I wanted them~~ for his birthday. They rival any fancy steakhouse's finest blades, and let me point out, they were not inexpensive.

"What are you doing?" I asked Joe one day shortly after the purchase, noticing he was unsetting the table I had just set.

"I'm just putting the new knives back and getting the old ones out," he said. "I want to save the good ones."

"For what?" I demanded.

"For company," he said.

My husband is the world's most gracious host, and I love that about him, I really do. I also wanted to use ~~my~~ . . . his fucking knives.

Here's the thing: My grandparents spent forty years sitting day in and day out on couches covered in plastic. This was in Florida, where humidity runs around 111 percent year round and ninety degrees in the summer is considered a "cool front," so I can only imagine that lounging on those condom-covered couches must have been like a visit to the tenth circle of hell in Dante's infamous *Inferno*. Gram and Gramp took the plastic off only when we came over, which I'm ashamed to admit wasn't that often. When they died—both well into their nineties—those ugly-ass greenish-gold brocade couches looked brand-spanking-new. It was the saddest thing I ever saw in my life. My grandfather had worked hard all of his life and probably saved up for those couches for a decade or longer. And for what? So somebody else could enjoy their fine finish a crappy handful of times?

I used this story to illustrate the fact that we should *use*

~~our~~ *his knives*, but Joe wasn't paying attention. At least I didn't think he was, until a recent evening when he whipped up some massive, mouth-watering T-bones. After the girls set the table, I noticed Joe replacing the old knives they'd chosen. *With the good ones.* He did look a little anxious every time he heard my knife make contact with my plate (I was dulling the blade, damn it!), but I pretended not to notice. When I die, I want those blades to be rusty, dull, and gnarled beyond recognition.

There's a difference, of course, between enjoying the things you already own and feverishly acquiring more. During a recent weeding-out session, I counted six sets of bedsheets for our master bed alone (and since I prefer one set above all of the rest, I generally strip, wash, and replace them without ever considering any of the alternatives). I have four different sets of bathroom towels, seven throw blankets in a trunk in my living room, and at least thirty different cookie sheets in various stages of dented disrepair taking over my pantry. Surveying this assortment, it occurred to me that maybe we already had enough. My suspicions were confirmed with my husband's generous help.

"We spend too much money," he said.

"What does '*too much money*' mean?" I asked. "That's sort of vague and ambiguous. Too much compared to whom?"

"Too much compared to what we make," he replied.

"Oh," I muttered. "How much too much?"

"Technically, we spend more than we make," he said simply.

Well, that couldn't be good. We were supposed to be building a nest egg,* and instead we were scrambling away our money as fast as—or apparently faster than—we could earn it. I was deeply depressed after this conversation, a condition that normally makes me want to dash straight to Nordstrom and buy something whimsical and fabulous. But obviously, I couldn't. Instead, I marched to my computer and attempted to craft a realistic plan for my financial future.

This was not an easy endeavor. After all, it wasn't like I was going to give up my highlights or stop buying organic half-and-half. (YOLO, you know?) And I knew for a fact my kids would wind up killing each other or me if I tried the old go-find-a-stick-to-play-with routine, so nixing all of their extra-curricular activities wasn't an option. But I *could* stop buying stuff I didn't need just because it was impossibly cute or on sale or both, couldn't I? Surely I could limit myself on my cell phone minutes and find a cheaper TV package. It would actually be a relief to cancel the half-dozen subscriptions I have to magazines that I never, ever read. And I definitely could try really hard to resist those "buy two widgets and get the third widget FREE" deals that aren't really deals when you only need a single widget. I could even try to pay for things occa-

---

* I actually looked up that term to see where it came from. The definition is "a real or artificial egg left in a nest to induce hens to lay eggs there." This makes it sound like when you sock away money it magnetically attracts more money to come hang out with it, which is hella awesome and now I *really* want a nest egg, damn it.

sionally with cash, a trick I've found turns me into the penniest-pinching bitch you ever saw.

After much agonizing, I came up with the outline of what I call Jenna's Plan for Financial Freedom (Or at Least Dying with Enough Money to Pay for My Own Funeral). I'm not shooting for millions here—let's be realistic, shall we?—but I certainly don't want my kids getting saddled with a bill for the car or the house I never got around to paying off. Without further ado, I present to you JPFFF (OALDWEMTPFMOF):

I Will Quit Justifying. Seeing as I am not Mother Teresa or a pediatric oncologist caring for thirty-seven special-needs foster children, I don't really "deserve" a new purse or a night out. Yes, I work hard and I'm a nice person, but as I tell my children all the time, life isn't fair. (Google "Jenny McCarthy in a bikini" if you're unsure about this.) When I am pining for the latest new thingamabob, I will go for a walk, write a novella, work on a cure for athlete's foot, or find another way to treat myself that doesn't involve spending money I should be saving. (I may need someone to come and sit on me from time to time, but I can figure out those details later.)

I Will Distinguish Wants From Needs. Maybe this comes naturally for you, but when a friend posts on Facebook, "Brittany is selling Girl Scout cookies so hit me up if you need any!" I have been known to falsely jump to the conclusion after searching my cupboards and determining that they are completely void of Girl Scout cookies that I, therefore, must need them. Alas, I do not. I also don't "need" a manicure, a blowout, or an extra-hot triple-shot no-foam latte, as lovely as all of these things indubitably are. I need food and toilet paper and tooth-paste. Most everything else is a want. I will learn the difference. (Again, this may involve some sort of restraint system or a lobotomy. In any case, I am sure it can be done.)

I Will Spend More Time on Pinterest. You think I'm being sarcastic, but that place is a gold mine of money-saving ideas. (It's also a label whore's worst nightmare because there you will find things like—I shit you not—a Louis Vuitton waffle maker that stamps the signature initial logo into your breakfast cakes, so proceed with caution if you can't resist de-signer clothes, accessories, or breakfast foods.) Even though I am not crafty,* I am going to become a homemade gift queen. I will make flavored dipping oils, granola, tea cup candles, snow globes, Christmas ornaments, refrigerator magnets, lip scrubs, scented soaps, log holders, bottle lamps, finger puppets, shaving cream, place mats, and maybe, if I'm feeling adven-turous, a Star Wars clock. I will use recycled Ball jars to put my homespun goodies in, and wrap them with scraps of cloth and old newspapers, just like those crafty Pinterest ladies do. I will feel both accomplished and smug.†

I Will Avoid My Enemies. And by "enemies" I am refer-ring, of course, to Target and Costco. I feel bad calling out two of my favorite stores on the planet, but the reality is that

---

* Feel free to check out my Pinterest craft board, aptly called Even Though I Am Not Crafty.

† I probably will never do any of this, but I really like it in theory, so I'm including it. Maybe you're more determined/industrious than I am.

I have never once gone through the checkout aisle at either of these places and not been utterly, shockingly appalled at the total. Honestly, how can a few basic necessities—a bag of rice, some dinner napkins, thirty-two rolls of packing tape, a fur-lined hoodie, chicken skewers for an army, Missoni legwarmers, a few thousand yards of wire-trimmed leopard ribbon, and a motorcycle—add up to so goddamned *much*? Oh my God, do you see what happened there? Seriously, I'll go in for mustard and laundry soap, and come out with $875 worth of shit I didn't need and apparently can't afford. Target and Costco may bill themselves as bargain centers, but instead of saving you money, they suck you in with their dollar bins and then get you drunk on free samples, and when you're totally high on *scoring a thousand acetaminophen for three bucks*, they stick a siphon into your wallet and suck everything out. If you're me, you're too busy enjoying a two-foot-long $1.50 hot dog to notice. But not anymore. I am onto these guys, and I will not get sucked in.*

I Will Recycle the Crap Out of Everything That Isn't People, Food, or Feces. Recycling saves money! It saves the earth! I can do it, too! I will stop buying those overpriced sticky notes, and instead stockpile scrap paper for writing notes and lists and printing recipes and test documents. I will fill up one of my many, many BPA-free water bottles with water from home before I head out so that I'm not stopping every hour to

---

* *As deeply or as often.*

buy another liquid refreshment. I will turn off lights when I am not using them and quit buying more produce than I know we can ever possibly eat. I will try to be like my frugal Little Grandma—a four-eleven slip of a thing thus dubbed to distinguish her from poor, towering Big Grandma—who made her own cat litter out of hand-shredded scraps of newspaper. (Except that would probably be a bitch to change and life *is* awfully short, so instead I will buy the dusty, generic scoopable cat litter instead of the nicely scented name-brand kind. My plan is nothing if not flexible!)

I Will Suck It Up and Have a Garage Sale. I know, I swore those off years ago, after a particularly bad one where a guy asked if the staple gun we were selling worked, and when I said yes, he put it up to the palm of his hand and pulled the trigger, dripping blood all over my twenty-five-cent T-shirt table. This was the same day that a nice old lady insisted I put five dollars' worth of batteries into the giant Talking Mother Goose to prove that it worked, and then took off with them after giving me a lousy dollar for the chatty bird. If that weren't bad enough, that evening—hours after the last of our unwanted castoffs had been hauled to Goodwill—this lady *came back with the goddamned goose,* insisting that it had stopped working. She handed it back to me and I gave her back her dollar, realizing only later that she'd pinched the damned batteries out of it. BUT STILL, I will have a garage sale, because as Deepak says, abundance can't come to you if there's no room for it to roost, or something like that.

I Will Remember That Money Isn't Everything. Sure, it can buy you cars and boobs and fabulous European vacations and, subsequently, some measure of happiness. But it can't buy true love or robust health or a sparkling personality or an ounce of class or a legitimate spot on any bestseller list*—all things I'd trade for a seven-digit bank balance any day of the year.

---

* According to *Forbes* it can buy you an ill-gotten spot there . . . but then you'd be a total douche bag.

CHAPTER 12

My Boss Is a Bitch: A Self-Employment Story

Women my age are in a unique position. Unlike our moms just a generation before us—who mostly didn't pursue careers and if they did, their choices were basically teacher or nurse— we were told that we could *be anything we wanted to be* when we grew up. (Except strippers or circus performers, which was confusing since our dads were such huge fans of both.) Nothing could stop us! Fulfilling careers, doting husbands, darling children, showcase homes, gourmet meals, exotic vacations: We could have it all. All we had to do was go to school, get good grades, and work really hard, and the gods of success and fortune and happiness would follow us around everywhere we went, pissing all over our heads.

Forty-some-odd years later, I'm going to have to call bullshit.

I realize this probably isn't a newsflash to you—the sad reality that we can't in fact have it all, at least not simultaneously—especially if you're a working mom. Having it all would mean our very young children would be welcome at work with us, all day every day, where we'd be encouraged to take frequent block-building and baby-yoga breaks. Oh, and naps. Lots of naps. Never, ever would a tiny person we pushed out of our vaginas (or had removed surgically through a man-made gash in our abdomens or flew to China to adopt) cling crying to our legs, begging us between snotty, heaving sighs, *Please don't go to work, please, Mommy, please*, and ripping a hole in our hearts and our last pair of decent stockings in the process. When our spawn got older, we wouldn't even have to ask permission to slip out of the office to attend one of their class plays or shuttle them to various doctor's appointments; the world would know and respect the fact that our first job, always and forever, was being someone's mother, and everyone would bow at our feet whenever we donned our Mom hats. When our beneficiaries got older still, our bosses would hand out hefty bonuses to help us cover our newly outrageous auto-insurance tabs and the cost of adding another cell phone to our family plans. Our husbands would do the bulk of the grocery shopping and housekeeping duties, of course, even though they would have fabulously satisfying jobs, too, because the universal understanding would be that our work was more important. We'd be paid the handsome salaries that we deserve—in addition to a generous clothing allowance—and we'd never, ever have to choose between getting a pedicure and getting a promotion.

What's that saying again? *Oh yeah. If ifs and buts were candy and nuts, we'd all have a merry Christmas.*

I love being a mom. As often as not, it's also truly, spectacularly, overwhelmingly hard. My paying job is a petal-strewn cakewalk compared to the duties of motherhood. I'm not saying that I choose to work so I can get away from my kids (although believe me, there have been days I've locked myself in the office under the guise of "work" and played Scramble with Friends just to get a bloody break from it all), because not working isn't a financial option for me or my family. I'm just saying it's a really good thing I love what I do.

My dad used to say it all the time: "Find a job you love, and you'll never work a day in your life." He was right, of course. I cherish everything about writing and feel beyond blessed to be able to make a living by pecking out words on a keyboard all day, sipping homemade lattes, and rarely being forced to change out of my furry leopard-print robe. I'm also privileged in the sense that the career I accidentally fell into produces something—books I can hide from my children (well, honestly) and magazine articles and online posts I can rip out or print and ~~also hide from my children~~ save for posterity. I regret nothing at all about my vocational choice, and yet lately, thanks to the shitty economy and that whole "spending more than we make" business and maybe a tiny bit of the is-this-all-there-is that accompanies perimenopause, I find myself wondering what I would do if I were forced to support myself in some other way.

Think about all of the possibilities. You can build bridges, dig ditches, lay bricks, train dogs, and save lives. You can teach, serve, speak, sell, create, lobby, haul, design, decorate, embalm, and engineer; you can pull rotten teeth, fix broken bones, crunch endless numbers, and market your own cocktail brand.* You can shake, bake, and sauté all manner of things, and if you're modestly skilled and reasonably good-looking enough, you might even get a TV show out of it. Unfortunately, I would be miserable at all of these jobs, not to mention countless others.

It turns out I am spectacularly *not* good at more things than I can count. I cannot catch a ball from even a few feet away to save my life. I am wretched at remembering names, faces, and where I parked my car at the grocery store. Apparently, I was born without the voice-volume-control thing other people seem to have, as I am frequently told that I am an exceptionally loud talker. I USE CAPS LOCK A LOT TO MAKE A POINT (See? I'm even a loud *typer*), even though I know it's collectively frowned upon. I vocabulize, which is a word I made up for the act of making up words (my kids refer to their earballs as if they are legit things). My eyes glaze over when I have to read directions, so I usually just throw them away and wing it. I cannot do that breathe-to-the-side move you need to master in order to swim laps, which sucks because swimming is the one exercise you can do when you are otherwise injured— and I am otherwise injured ALL THE TIME. I have the pa-

---

* I am currently working on one myself. I'm thinking of calling it Undernourished Female Dog. Has a nice ring, right?

tience of a kid waiting in line to get into Disneyland, I curse like a drunken sailor prone to stubbing his toe every few minutes, and my husband calls me Grace . . . because I don't have any. Oh, and trust me when I tell you that you've never seen an uglier cookie, pie, or cake than one that I've attempted to bake. This isn't *everything* I suck at, of course, but it gives you an idea of how hard switching careers would be for me.

I asked Joe what other jobs he could see me doing. He thought about it for sixteen years.

"What about, like, somebody who teaches parrots to talk?" he suggested finally. "Is that a thing?"

"Are you serious?" I asked. "*Training parrots* is the only thing you can think of that I might be good at doing?"

"Well, you know, you do talk a lot . . ."

"Women in general talk a lot, dear," I explained. "Should we all be parrot trainers?"

"Maybe," he said seriously.

"How many talking parrots do you suppose we need in this world?" I demanded.

"Probably not that many," he agreed.

I asked my friend Tanya the same question. Thankfully, she didn't have to think about it for an eternity, and she didn't say a *fucking parrot trainer*.

"You could work at one of those high-end furniture stores telling them where to put the stuff!" she yelled, all excited.

"Is that a job?" I asked.

"Totally," she insisted. "I think they're called stagers. You'd be the person telling the other people, like, put the carpet at this angle and these knickknacks would look fantastic over here. You'd be awesome at that!"

"So I'd be awesome at bossing people around?" I asked.

"Yes!" she said. "But you know, in a really thoughtful and creative way."

I put a query out to my Facebook friends and was only slightly depressed by the responses: Drill sergeant. (Ouch.) Baptist minister. (I'm pretty sure they aren't allowed to drink. Next.) Stand-up comedian. (Is "sit-down comedian" a thing? Because anything with "stand-up" in the title sounds exhausting.) Sex-toy boutique owner. (Because I have a porn-star name, *obviously.*) Counselor. But only for people who can take the truth. (*Professional* jerk. Perfect!) Product tester at Trader Joe's. (What does this mean, exactly? Like, I could sample the lemon scones and curry simmer sauces and wasabi peas, and then tell people if they're good or not? What if I hated everything? What if I loved everything and nobody else did? I couldn't handle the pressure.)

After much soul-searching, I have determined that the only other career that I think I might have any degree of success at is being a professional organizer. Because not to brag or anything, but I can organize the shit out of pretty much anything. Doing it wouldn't feel like work to me; in fact, I've been known to *beg* friends to let me sort through their closets and tidy up their files. But I know from experience—and by experience I mean the time I took home the entire second grade Math Tiles system and organized it within an inch of its life, only to watch the thing go right to hell in a handbasket within a matter of days—that my painstaking services would almost certainly go to waste. You can lead a horse to a nice, clean watering trough, but that filthy SOB will turn it into a slobbery mess before you can say, "Secretariat takes the crown."

I remember reading an article years ago that featured a group of women who had all begun entirely new careers after fifty. One woman, who'd finally realized her dream of graduating from medical school, told of the pivotal moment in her life that had launched her journey. Her adult son had asked her what she would be doing if she could do anything in the world. She told him without question she'd be a doctor. When he scoffed and asked why she wasn't doing it *now*, she reminded him that she'd be fifty-two when she graduated from med school. "You're going to be fifty-two anyway," he'd reminded her gently.

Sort of makes you think, huh?

If all of the career limitations in the world—time and money and TV-star good looks and competing against a younger, smarter, skinnier field of applicants—went away, what on earth would I want to do with my time all day long? Open an Etsy shop? Be somebody's personal shopper? Nurse motherless lion cubs to robust health? *Why was this so fucking hard?*

"I'm going to go to beauty school," my pal Ellie announced recently. Ellie is a spectacularly talented painter, musician, and photographer who has traveled and worked around the world. A classic starving artist, Ellie has decided that she would very much enjoy the luxury of continuing to eat and having a roof over her head, so she's been searching for a new career. She toyed with the ideas of becoming a psychotherapist, a high school French teacher, or a scuba instructor, finally settling on becoming a hairstylist. *At our age.*

"You don't have the wet-hair-in-the-drain thing?" I asked. I have a pretty touchy gag reflex to begin with, but when I have to scoop hair out of a sink or shower drain, it is absolutely all I can do not to puke. Even if it's my own hair I'm retrieving. I am pretty sure that would make me a lousy hairdresser. That and if I had to stand on my feet all damned day long—in seven-inch stilettos, which seem to be required hairdresser footwear, at least at my hair salon—I'd be in one of those *Sixteen Candles* back braces within a month. And also, because I have a hard time not being really blunt, I can see a whole lot of this happening:

CLIENT: *[Holding up a picture of Reese Witherspoon]* I'd like my hair to look like this.

ME: Hahahahaha, wouldn't we all!

CLIENT: *[Storming out of the salon in tears]*

ME: Anybody have a parrot that needs training?

The idea of teaching appeals to me in a way—you know, you get to talk a *lot* when you're a teacher—so maybe I could teach writing. Or organizing. Or sarcasm. Then I remembered that I learned in college that just because you're proficient at something doesn't mean you're good at showing other people how to do it. I was sailing through my math classes, and my professor suggested I sign up as a tutor in the math lab. It would be an easy three credit hours, he promised. It might even be fun.

It was not fun.

ME: If X plus Y equals Z, and X equals 10 and Z equals 15, what is Y?

SUICIDAL STUDENT: A letter in the alphabet?

ME: I can't help you.

Another friend, Amy, was thrust back into the workplace after an unexpected and particularly ugly divorce left her broke and desperate. Despite the fact that Amy has multiple degrees and a resume so impressive you half want to ask her to prove it's real, she was passed over for a parade of jobs that were given to younger, less-experienced candidates. After months of searching and being told repeatedly that she was overqualified for every position she applied for (*overqualified* is the politically correct term for "we can get someone way younger to do it for much less"), Amy finally landed a job as a personal assistant. Her boss is ten years younger than she is, has more money than an oil baron (he's vague on where his money comes from, so maybe he *is* an oil baron), and likes her to wear really short skirts to work.

I told her he was a pig.

"If he wanted me to prance around in crotchless chaps and was willing to give me health benefits, I'd consider it," Amy insisted. Apparently, the pickings are that slim.

It's not always outright necessity that causes people to have midlife career crises. Sometimes you just wake up and realize you've been doing the same miserable, mirthless, unfulfilling thing for the last twenty years, and if you don't do something about it now, you'll be doing it for the *next* twenty years. My friend Winn, who'd fallen into the family financial planning business right after college, had this very epiphany recently and immediately enrolled in nursing school. She'll be knocking on fifty's door when she puts on that sassy white uniform for the very first time. Is she daunted at all by this?

"Hell no!" she shouted when I asked her. In fact, Winn insists that at least thirty of the forty students in her program are our age *or older*. "The coolest thing about going back to school at our age is that you actually give a shit about learning this time," she added. "It's not just about which guys in your class you want to have sex with. Although there is that, too."

"Do you ever think about quitting?" I asked her.

"Once you're committed to something at this point in your life, it's like you're pregnant with it," she told me. "I can't uncommit now. I've taken ten thousand dollars' worth of classes! Besides, I don't think it matters how old you are when you get there. Sam Walton was forty-four when he opened the first Walmart. Frank McCourt wrote *Angela's Ashes* in his late sixties. Look, it's not like any of us are ever going to see any money from Social Security, so it's stupid to think we're going to be able to *retire* or anything. I'm thinking if I'm going to be working for another thirty or forty years, it damn well better be something I like doing."

Danish philosopher Søren Kierkegaard said, "Life must be

lived forwards, but can only be understood backwards." What he means by this, I'll take the liberty of translating, is that *you can't possibly know what you want to do for the rest of your life until you've already done it.* When you're young and naïve and career-hunting for the first time, the entire world is like one huge menu. Lots of the options sound deliciously enticing, but many of them don't live up to the hype. (Let's face it: Parisian-style steak tartare could also be called raw cow flesh topped with pickled shrub parts.) My husband, for instance, who loves everything sporty and adventurous,* many years ago decided to build his own outdoor adventure company from scratch. He devoted ten years of his life to this endeavor, and it became quite successful. And do you know what he realized after an entire decade of grueling, ground-up work? That there wasn't anything at all sporty or adventurous about sitting behind a desk designing fabulous excursions for other people to enjoy.

It was a bittersweet day when he finally shuttered that business. He was happy not to be a full-time paper-pusher anymore, but he also spent several months mourning the death of the dream, the one where he'd spend his days leading eager clients to the top of breathtaking mountain peaks in Pakistan and racing sled dogs in Alaska and whitewater rafting with crocodiles in Africa (which incidentally kills an average of thirty people a year, according to *AskMen*, "mostly from

---

* You may recall from previous books that the man I married is fond of camping—whereas I'm intensely fond of *not camping*—and is still trying to get me to try something called spelunking.

crocodiles," so I was slightly less morose about burying this dream than he was).

Some people, like me, get lucky in those early days and quite by accident pick something they turn out to love doing; others, like Joe, get sort of screwed. They suffer through years of schooling or decades of corporate-ladder scaling and then finally land their "dream job" only to realize it's more of a nightmare. The choices then are to suck it up or get the hell out and start over. Sure, starting from scratch—and being the low (wo)man on the totem pole *again* and possibly answering to a boss you are old enough to have birthed—might be a bitch. But I have to agree with the brilliant businesswoman and pioneering comedienne Lucille Ball who said, "I'd rather regret the things I've done than regret the things I haven't done."

So if this writing thing doesn't pan out, I will forge onward. Look me up if you ever need a parrot trainer.

CHAPTER 13

Complaining about How Tired I Am Is Exhausting

When I was little, both sets of grandparents lived nearby,* and we kids would occasionally have sleepovers at their houses. (Presumably, this was so my parents could get drunk and have sex without having to worry about us barging in on them, but if it's all the same, I'd rather not dwell on that.) While my mom's parents had the traditional king-size bed setup, my dad's parents slept in far-apart twin beds. I was a huge fan of both *I Love Lucy* and *The Dick Van Dyke Show* at the time, so I didn't think this was all that odd. Plus everyone knew that my dad's

---

* This was in the olden days when you only had two sets—your mom's parents and your dad's—and not the thirteen you get to acquire today through countless divorces and remarriages.

mom had serious issues with sleep. She made it abundantly clear, as she tucked our little PJ-clad bodies into the pullout sofa bed, that if we made even the tiniest audible peep during the night, it would ruin any hope of her catching a single additional Z for the rest of the evening, and then her wide-awake ass would be forced to stab us to death with her knitting needles. Oh, those weren't her *exact* words, but you'd better believe the threat was there.

(True story: Those same grandparents had a framed picture in their bathroom with this heartwarming inscription: "Yea, though I walk through the valley of the shadow of death, I shall fear no evil, for I am the meanest sonofabitch in the valley." Yes, this elegant bit of artwork lived *in my grandparent's bathroom*, where a kid could enjoy its uplifting wisdom every time she went in there to relieve her bladder or bowels. You really can't make this shit up. I do think it explains a lot, though.)

At the time, I thought her sleep weirdness was just one of those quirky Grandma things, like cheek pinching and tomato stewing and bobby pinning my bangs off of my face the minute I walked through her front door. But recently I realized that my grandmother wasn't much older than I am now when I was born. She wasn't some eccentric old lady with an unusually low threshold for midnight wake-up calls or an undiagnosed sleep disorder. She was middle-aged, hormonal, exhausted, married to a snorer, and probably fantasized daily about finally getting enough shut-eye that she'd wake up refreshed and well-rested, and not have gigantic bags under her eyes. She was me.

I really hate admitting it, but pretty much every human encounter I have starts like this:

OTHER PERSON: Hey, Jenna! How are you?
ME: Oh my God, *I'm exhausted.* How are you?

I'm exhausted, of course, for a million reasons. I have children. We have cats and dogs. My brain never shuts off. I'm a compulsive neat freak so when other people are relaxing or enjoying a nice TV show or book on a quiet evening,* I'm wiping out the crisper drawers in the refrigerator or organizing all of the Monopoly cards so that they face the same way in the box. My husband snores. Our neighbors fight, loudly and often. There's a nest of the most obnoxiously vocal birds God ever created about four feet from my bedroom window, and those chirpy motherfuckers insist on belting out the song of their congregation from sundown to sunup with absolutely no regard for decency or day parts.

Health magazines and websites suggest my problem also could be my thyroid, midlife hormones, not enough exercise/water/vegetables, too much stress/caffeine/alcohol, or too few massages. Okay, fine, they never say the part about the massages, but come on! I can't be the only one who tosses and turns at all hours of the night but is fully passed out fifteen minutes into any hour that I'm paying someone seventy-five bucks to touch me. Surely I am onto something here.

---

* And by "other people" I mean "my husband."

I've upgraded my bed and all of its accessories—twice—thinking that if I could somehow replicate the conditions of that delicious hotel bed I slept in like a comatose sloth,* routine sound slumber would be mine. Instead, I regularly lie in my elegantly appointed, impossibly plush overpriced cocoon and calculate how many more years of toiling I'm going to have to put in before the thing is fully paid off.

Try drugs, you shout. With all due respect, do you think I am a complete moron? If it's reported or even suggested to help a person drift off, I've swallowed, slurped, or smoked it.† Lunesta, Sonata, Ambien, Nyquil, Melatonin, Unisom, Sominex, Rescue Remedy, chamomile tea, a fifth of Jack Daniel's, a big fat joint; none of them have brought me blissful unconsciousness. Well, except the dope, but I think it's safe to say I'm not really stoner material. I'm not much of a snacker, I don't like the smell or the taste, and not to be all judgey or anything but I don't think nightly toking would be setting the best-ever example for my daughters. ("Okay, girls, Mommy's just going to take a nice big bong hit and go to bed. You guys be sure to brush your teeth really well, okay? And remember, just say no to drugs!")

---

* Let's all agree to stop using the expression "slept like a baby," unless we're referring to a drunken occasion where we piss ourselves, scream and cry fitfully for no apparent reason every thirty minutes, and wake with one of our limbs wedged through the slats of the headboard, okay?

† I smoked it one time, before a Ziggy Marley concert. I passed out cold and missed the show. To this day my husband thinks it is hilarious to point out that I am possibly the only person in all of ever who can say she was too high to go to a *Ziggy Marley concert.*

A little side note about sleeping pills. Remember when Kerry Kennedy, ex-wife of New York governor Andrew Cuomo and quasi-famous daughter of Robert and Ethel, was arrested on suspicion of DUI after she was found slumped over the wheel of her car in the wee hours of the morning? Turns out the incident was caused by "Ambien-induced sleep driving," which apparently is a common side effect of the drug that leads people to *get into their cars and drive them while they are asleep*, often without any memory of the events. It sounds like pure bullshit, except I know that it's not because it happened to my friend Anna.

Anna didn't drive anywhere, though. But after popping an Ambien, without having any idea she was doing it, she padded to her computer and sent a Facebook message to a cute guy she'd met recently, asking him out on a date. (Fortunately, Anna was single at the time.) She didn't stop there, either. She then found some stationery and a pen—she was dead asleep at the time, I'll remind you—and wrote this gentleman a nice handwritten note (expressing her passionate desire for him, of course), which she proceeded to address, stamp, and place carefully into her mailbox before returning to bed.

Imagine Anna's surprise when her secret crush called to thank her for the extremely zealous letter she had no memory of writing or sending.

"He's offered to show it to me several times, but I think I'd rather not see it," Anna says. The two are now friends, which is what usually happens when one person has some mortifying, incriminating evidence on the other.

Anyway, I probably don't need Ambien anyway, as falling asleep isn't the biggest issue for me. More often than not I can accomplish that part without too much unnecessary stress or pharmaceutical intervention. But when anything wakes me up—my beloved's snoring, an ambulance siren a half mile away, run-of-the-mill axe-murder nightmares, remembering I forgot to mail a friend's birthday card, one of my cats emitting her long, low, I've-captured-a-lizard-for-you-because-I-love-you-deeply-now-where-would-you-like-me-to-leave-its-headless-entrails moan—I'm up for the duration. Every time I complain about this in the morning, my husband says the same thing:

"Why didn't you wake me up?" he demands. Of course, he means for sex. Because naturally *he* has no problem falling or staying asleep, ever.

"I would bloody fucking *kill* you if you woke me up in the middle of the night just because you were awake," I tell him.

"Do I have to remind you that we're different, Jenna?" he sighs. "Let me say it again: You can wake me up *anytime you want, multiple times in a single evening for the rest of your life,* if it means we can have sex."

Is it bad that I'd rather have the sleep?

At least I'm not alone. A study by the National Sleep Foundation found that more than half of surveyed respondents would pick an epic night of sleep over a mind-blowing shag. (A decade ago, only 31 percent of us were more fatigued than frisky.) The same study found that 61 percent of us admit that our omnipresent cell phones are a big part of the problem, and

I know this to be true because once, during a bout of insomnia, I texted a friend a funny cartoon I'd found on my iFunny app.

Hahaha, but what the fuck are you doing awake at 3:30 a.m.? she texted me right back.

I can't sleep, I wrote, surprised to get a reply. Why are YOU awake?

I WASN'T AWAKE! she shouted back at me, all-caps style. SO THANKS FOR BRINGING ME DOWN WITH YOU.

Here's a thought, I replied, pecking angrily at my tiny screen with two fingers and cursing the moron who designed the iPhone's dysfunctional keyboard. TURN YOUR GODDAMNED RINGER OFF!

She texted me back something highly unprintable.

So I'm the asshole here because YOU keep your ringer on all night and I'm supposed to know this? I wasn't about to let this go. Plus I was wide awake and had nothing better to do.

She must have gone back to sleep at this point. Lucky bitch.

I'm starting to think exhaustion might be the new global pandemic, like scarlet fever or the black plague or swarms of locusts were way back when. Pretty much everyone I know is running on fumes. My friend Michelle has decided that she absolutely has chronic fatigue syndrome, a self-diagnosis she arrived at after coming to the startling realization that she is fatigued pretty much chronically. No matter how many hours of sleep she logs, Michelle insists she can fall asleep anytime, anywhere, and that she never feels fully rested. Her doctor suggested regular, painful Vitamin B shots and a daily bowlful of supplements.

"Notice any difference?" I asked a few weeks into her new routine.

"My pee is neon," she yawned.

All of this exhaustion is not good for us. For starters, sleep deprivation is known to play a role in everything from heart attacks and high blood pressure to strokes and diabetes. (Of course, so is stress, so try not to get too freaked by all of that if you're a lousy sleeper.) Too little sleep also impairs critical thinking and motor coordination, and has been linked to high-profile accidents including the Exxon *Valdez* oil spill, the Chernobyl nuclear meltdown, and the Three Mile Island disaster. As worrisome as that may be, I have to say it makes me feel better about splashing half-and-half all over the counter every morning in a sluggish daze.

Not so happy with what you're seeing in the mirror lately? Blame that evasive Sandman. Those hours when we're supposedly drifting peacefully through Dreamland are specifically designated for cellular repair and renewal. Fail to log enough shut-eye, and we're left with dull, puffy skin and a halo of dilated blood vessels around our eyes. When insomnia becomes a chronic problem, forget about beauty sleep; nothing short of a medically induced beauty coma can help.

We're our own harshest critics though, right? I mean, nobody else even notices your slack skin or swollen, bloodshot eyes, do they? Actually, they do. In one interesting Swedish study, researchers photographed a group of participants twice, once after logging eight solid hours of sleep and again after they were limited to five hours of rest. The researchers then asked a group of unwitting observers to rate the participants on how healthy and attractive they were in each set of photos. Across the board, the sleepy group was ranked far lower on almost every positive attribute imaginable. Are you getting the gist of this? People were labeling complete strangers sick and ugly after a measly three-hour sleep deficit.

I know, now you're depressed. But wait, it gets even worse. If you're sleepy and notice you've also been packing on a few unwanted pounds, it's probably no coincidence. When we're fatigued, our bodies are hardwired to seek out the pleasure response unique to consuming massive quantities of food. (This is probably one of those evolutionary protection measures, like our nervous systems assume we are so mind-numbingly tired because we're being chased by a pack of saber-toothed tigers, so we'd better hurry up and eat something so we have enough energy to get away!) At the same time, the stress hormones that are released when we're under-rested cause our pancreases to crank out insulin, which is also unkindly referred to as the "fat-storage hormone." In other words, when we're dragging ass, we're actually encouraging our asses to stockpile fat so that they drag even farther and lower. Talk about irony.

There has to be a solution, I plead with my friend Google.

Try me, Google says.

So I search online—for the fifth or sixth billionth time—for "guaranteed sleep solution," because there has to be one. People devote their entire lives to figuring out all sorts of nagging little conundrums. In the past year alone scientists have cured blindness and epilepsy in mice, grown viable teeth from stem cells, and discovered that chimpanzees solve puzzles for fun, just like humans. Surely somebody has been working on a pill or potion that will help us all do something that is supposed to come naturally but frequently, frustratingly doesn't. I'm not asking to be turned into a hibernating bear; I'd just love to drift quickly and peacefully into unconsciousness, stay there for seven or eight consecutive hours, and then wake up perky and refreshed. Is that really too much to ask, Google?

I search and I search and I even set up alerts in case there's a breakthrough in the middle of the night and I miss it because I'm very busy watching the numbers on my alarm clock blink. Most of what I find is about as helpful as "try to get more sleep," a recommendation that sort of makes me want to punch the advice giver in the esophagus. Here's a sampling of some of the best suggestions the sleep experts are doling out:

Don't drink alcohol right before bed. I'm not sure how drinking earlier in the day is going to help me sleep better, but I'm willing to try it.

Reduce stress. Oh my God, why didn't I think of this? I'll just quit my job, stop worrying about saving for retirement, and put my kids up for adoption. I'm feeling sleepy just thinking about it.

Buy room-darkening blinds. Seeing as I get up long before the sun does every day, I am not convinced this will help me. But any excuse to redecorate—especially in the name of health and beauty—is always welcome, so I vow to start trolling Overstock.com immediately for sassy new window treatments.

Limit exercise for at least three hours before bedtime. Well, if they *insist*.

Have a nice snack before turning in. Supposedly, a mini-meal that contains both carbohydrates and protein an hour or two before bed triggers your brain to produce the calming neurotransmitter serotonin. And since that sounds highly scientific and also I do love a good grilled cheese sandwich in bed, I am definitely going to try this one.

Don't overdo the snacking. On the other hand, going to bed with *too much* food in your stomach is a recipe for restlessness, the pros say. Clearly these assholes have never experienced the joy of shoveling four heaping platefuls of Thanksgiving dinner and a generous sampling of dessert into their pieholes and then falling into a deeply satisfying coma. *Don't buy this one, you guys.* I say, eat up for better sleep!

Limit daytime napping. Hahahahahaha. Seriously, am I four? The last time I took a nap was about five years ago, after pulling an all-nighter on the bathroom floor during a nasty stomach flu episode. But thanks for the hot tip, sleep experts. Did you learn this in medical school?

Unplug your clock. Well, this one is just flat-out ridiculous. If I unplugged my clock, how on *earth* would I know how late it was and then calculate the bare-minimum amount of critical rapid eye movement sleep I would get if I fell asleep *this very minute*, which of course I won't? I guess I could always check my cell phone, since I sleep with that thing under my pillow. *With the ringer off,* of course.

Do not sleep with your cell phone under your pillow. WTF?

Avoid bright lights before bed. So you're saying that I shouldn't turn all of the lamps in the house on full power at night as part of my relaxing, presleep ritual? Next you're going to tell me I shouldn't drink an after-dinner espresso!

Limit caffeine. See "avoid bright lights before bed."

Practice good "sleep hygiene." Which sounds like "don't go to bed dirty," but apparently, it means you should stick to the same bedtime schedule on weekends and vacations as you do during the regular workweek. I'm happy to report that my insomnia does not own a calendar, so I already do this! Yay!

Let it go. This is not actual, professional advice, but honestly, it's pretty much all we can do. We'll sleep when we're dead. In the meantime, the next time you're staring at your alarm clock and seeing if you can predict *precisely* when the number is going to flip, why not roll on top of your partner and give him or her a little midnight-special surprise? You may or may not pass out immediately afterward but fifty bucks says the trash will get taken out the next day *without you even having to ask.* It's worth a shot.

·····················

CHAPTER 14

Please Don't Make Me
Run with Bulls

I am not lying when I tell you that until a year or two ago, I had never even heard of the term "bucket list." Then all of a sudden I started seeing them all over Pinterest, and while I could tell these posts were some sort of extremely ambitious to-do lists, the term was confusing to me. What did climbing Kilimanjaro or learning Mandarin Chinese have to do with mopping a floor or milking a cow? I Googled *bucket list* and discovered that apparently there was a movie of the same name, directed by the brilliant Rob Reiner and starring the incomparable duo of Jack Nicholson and Morgan Freeman. In the flick—which I am pretty sure I haven't seen, but I have been known to forget entire movies before the credits are finished rolling, so don't hold it against me if I'm wrong—two dying

·············

men meet in the hospital and then set off on a raucous road trip with a list of things each wants to do before he, as it's been so eloquently put, kicks the bucket.

That sort of made sense, but because I'm a dork I got to thinking about the phrase itself—again, what was the link?—so I kept digging. It turns out there are two competing theories regarding the origin of the expression. The most widely held one maintains that the saying came from the practice of hanging oneself, ostensibly by standing on a bucket to reach the noose, and then quite literally "kicking the bucket" away and effectively sealing the deal. I'm suspicious of this explanation, I have to admit. I mean how many people just happen to have a bunch of big, sturdy, empty buckets lying around when the urge to hang themselves strikes? Or even just one? If I wanted to kill myself in this particularly gruesome manner, I think I'd choose a chair or a ladder to hoist myself up to the rope rather than having to go out to the garage and dump a bunch of crap out of this bucket or that one and then hope that the damned thing wouldn't crack as soon as I stepped up onto it. In fact, I'd pick pretty much anything over a bucket for this purpose: a durable wooden crate, a small stool, or even an end table would do. But I guess "kick the stackable-step-aerobics thingy" doesn't have quite the same ring.

The other theory is that the phrase has to do with the wooden frame—also known as a bucket—used to hang animals by their feet for slaughter. In this uplifting and incredibly visual scenario, desperate, dying animals invariably "kick the bucket" as they lose the struggle for their lives. How this could have reached the tipping point of entering the vernacular is beyond me. "Hey, Bobby, did you see that sonofabitch kick the bucket? I hope *I* never kick the bucket, if you know what I mean."

Whatever the case, the phrase came from somewhere, and now—thanks to the Internet in general and the great time-suck that is Pinterest in particular—everybody knows what a bucket list is. Lots of people I know even have one. I feel like a colossal slacker for saying this, but I do not have a bucket list. Probably because I don't even like thinking about dying in the peripheral sense, so any such list I had would probably be boringly short: "Don't kick the bucket, the end."

Aside from preferring to remain in denial about my mortality, I also am a prolific list maker. Because of this I have an issue with the part where as soon as you write something down, you're sort of bound to it. If I made a list of things I wanted to do and then impulsively put, for instance, "run a marathon" on it, I'd be haunted by guilt every single day that I didn't run, which would be every single day because I hate running and I have really bad feet and an even worse back, and besides I can't run without music but I can't find my iPod charger *or* my earbuds, and who the fuck has time to run dozens of miles a week, and also, did I mention that I hate running?

Apparently, it's a midlife rite of passage, though, this crafting of the highly specific inventory of things you want to do before you are permanently out of print. And people post their intentions right on the Internet, where anyone can see them and everyone on the planet can hold them accountable. The

Pinterest-style lists are usually short and sweet (visit Mount Rushmore, stand under the Hollywood sign, see a Broadway show), but if you search for bucket list blogs, you will not believe how into this shit people can be. One blogger-guy I found had fifty things on his list. Fifty! Sure, some of them (such as eat caviar and buy a stranger a meal) could be ticked off in a matter of minutes, but at least a third of them (including learn a new language and then speak it fluently, write a screenplay, and design and sell a line of T-shirts) could take months, even years to accomplish. How does this guy even know he has that much time? Does he realize that if he dropped dead tomorrow, he'd be leaving behind an itemized inventory of his failures? As if those things weren't discouraging enough, that bastard had the *huevos* to put *make a difference* on his bucket list! I mean, how exactly is he going to know when *that* item is ready for a strike-through?

"Let's see, last month I flew in a helicopter and learned how to juggle, and today I made a difference. *[Draws a fat line through each of these items smugly.]* I sure am glad I made this bucket list!"

The more lists I found, the more daunted I became by the whole prospect. Another guy's list had one hundred travel-related items alone, an itinerary I couldn't help mentally calculating the cost of and wondering what the hell this dude does for a living that he could even consider pursuing them all. (Assume he's forty-five and will be fit and healthy enough for adventure travel until he's seventy-five. That's still more than three major vacations every year to such exotic locales as

Dubai, Dublin, Antarctica, and the Amazon jungle, to name a few.) The guy dreams of going Zorbing in New Zealand;* I fantasize about getting all-over laser hair removal and having sprinklers installed in my front yard.

I wondered if not having a bucket list meant I was lazy or uninspired. Although I don't typically use my husband as a barometer of normalcy, I asked Joe if he had one.

"Not really," he said.

"Well, if you had one, what would be on it?" I wanted to know.

"Lots of stuff," he replied.

"Name two things," I urged.

"Climb Machu Picchu and circumnavigate the Channel Islands on a kayak," he articulated easily.

"Oh," I said. "Yeah, I don't really want to do either of those things. You know, one guy has 'make a difference' on his bucket list."

"I make a difference every day," Joe said. "I break at a yellow light instead of plowing through it and the guy behind me has to stop, too? Bam! I just made a difference."

This, of course, is one of the many reasons I love my husband.

What *do* I want to do before I die? I don't have the urge to scale, climb, or cross that many things. I don't want to be chased by bulls, shake a president's hand, or have my picture

---

* Apparently Zorbing is a popular down under "sport" that involves climbing into a large transparent ball and then being pushed down hills. I do not want to do this, ever.

taken with the Pope. I'm not interested in skydiving, bungee jumping, seeing the Jell-O museum,* or riding the subway without pants, which apparently is a dream some people feel compelled to realize before they buy the cardboard condo. My list would be much more amorphous (and if I'm being honest, far less aerobic): Be an honorable wife, mother, friend, and person. Have enough money to pay for my funeral. Top a bestseller list. Be part of a flash mob. Don't die.

"Maybe you don't need a bucket list because you've already done so many cool things," my friend Kim insisted. "You've lived in New York, you speak French, you have tattoos, and you've flown in a helicopter . . . You never wrote any of that down; it just happened. I'm sure you'll do plenty more awesome stuff before you d—I mean, you know, whenever."

Kim was right. I'm not rich and I'm far from famous,† but I have had some cool jobs and traveled to some amazing places and lived in some badass cities (even though my view in most of them amounted to a *Laverne & Shirley*–style view of passersby's feet). The more I thought about what I'd already done and where I'd already been, the clearer my new purpose became: I needed

---

* Yes, there is one. It's actually called the Jell-O Gallery, and it's in Le Roy, NY—also known as the "birthplace of Jell-O"—and you guys, there are people on this earth who do not want to die without having visited it. The mind boggles.

† Although I I *do* occasionally get recognized on the street and in Costco. Sadly, it's almost always from the house-flipping show my husband and I appeared on and not from my TED talk or any of my books.

to make a *backward* bucket list! Sure it's nice to have hopes and goals and dreams for the future, but it's also important to take a moment to sit back and reflect on ~~the totally crazy shit~~ the many things you've already achieved, experienced, or survived. This is a perfect exercise for someone like me because I *really* like crossing stuff off of my to-do lists. So whenever I'm feeling like a loser/slacker, I can print a copy of my BBL and systematically scratch through every last item on it. Brilliant, right?

So far, my BBL has the following fun and occasionally insane accomplishments on it:

1. Climb a frozen waterfall*

2. Push two basketball-sized babies out of my vagina without requiring follow-up surgery or dying

3. Buy a one-way plane ticket and move from one coast to the other all by myself for no other reason than "I'm tired of being cold"

4. Swim with dolphins

5. Ride in an elevator with uber-scary *Vogue* editor-in-chief Anna Wintour and not shit myself

6. Accept a coveted staff writing job at a national New York magazine despite having zero skills or experience and without asking the salary

---

* I once *did* have the urge to scale things, but it was fleeting.

7. Become a popular FM radio DJ despite having zero skills or experience and knowing full well the salary

8. Have a huge poster of my DJ face on the back of buses all over town

9. Pump breast milk on the air

10. Ask Paul Reiser to endorse one of my books*

11. Shag golf balls for a summer at Pebble Beach

12. Be interviewed by Khloé Kardashian on the *TODAY* show

13. Take surfing lessons

14. Interview Dave Barry

15. Get a tattoo in Amsterdam

16. Skinny-dip in the ocean at night

17. Copilot (okay, sit in the copilot seat) of a single engine, two-passenger plane

18. Enjoy a famous Mardi Gras Fat Tuesday parade multiple times and remember it

19. Pose for a full-size, full-color photo spread in a national magazine alongside the headline "I Was a Slut for a Day"

---

* I did ask—I have a copy of the letter to prove it. He just never responded. *Obviously* my letter got lost in the mail. Paul, I totally forgive you!

20. Pay for a stranger's groceries

21. Stand in the attic where Anne Frank wrote her legendary diary

22. Ice-skate in Rockefeller Center

23. Drive from Florida to New York in a rented van with five cats

24. Scuba dive with sharks, like, *on purpose*

25. Drive a stick shift

26. Lay out on a topless beach

27. Make snow angels in Yosemite National Park

28. Ride a horse bareback alongside a highway

29. Beat someone at Ping-Pong

30. Buy a fixer-upper house and renovate it on TV

31. Hike through a Hawaiian rain forest

32. Convince my husband to take ballroom dancing lessons with me

33. Spend a week living like a baroness in a friend's ridiculously posh Manhattan penthouse

34. Make really good homemade gnocchi*

---

* Don't pooh-pooh that if you haven't done it. That shit is *not* easy to make.

35. See a burlesque show—with topless dancers and alligator wrestling and everything—at the Moulin Rouge

36. Fly in the same first-class cabin to Europe as Rod Stewart

37. Hitchhike in Paris*

38. Pitch a TV show, *Seinfeld*-style, to a room full of network executives

39. Watch a NASCAR race from the pit

40. Be plucked from the Blue Man Group audience to participate in the show

41. Pick up tennis as an adult and become modestly proficient at it

42. Drive on the "wrong" side of the road in Ireland

43. Have dinner with Miramax co-founder and power producer Harvey Weinstein

44. Attend a photo shoot at the famous South Fork Ranch from the TV show *Dallas*

45. Go on a date with a D-list actor (Skippy from *Family Ties*, in case you're wondering)

46. Debate capital punishment in French

---

* I know, this wasn't very smart, and I'm lucky to be alive.

47. Practice sunrise yoga on a beach in the West Indies

48. Ride in a lawn chair in the back of a pickup truck*

49. Appear in a bathtub in a YouTube video promoting one of my books

50. Don't die

Look at that, would you? That's fifty mostly awesome things I've *already accomplished*, Mr. Make a Difference Blogger Guy. And I'm only forty-five! Imagine what my BBL is going to look like in another forty-five years. I just hope it has "participate in a flash mob" and "don't die" on it.

---

* I know, this wasn't very smart either, and I'm lucky to be alive.

CHAPTER 15

Newsflash: Steve Miller Isn't Cool Anymore

Bouncers ask for IDs to check to see if someone is old enough to get responsibly hammered inside their places of employment, but I think there's a way you can undeniably tell someone's age: Check out their iTunes library.

(Hint: If yours is overrun with titles by the Carpenters, Cheap Trick, Fleetwood Mac, Simon and Garfunkel, Rush, or the Bee Gees, you should probably consider purchasing long-term health insurance coverage sooner rather than later.)

When it comes to music, I swear I used to be cool. I was front and center when Madonna's very first Virgin Tour came to town, dressed of course in piles of neon jewelry layered over the sluttiest, laciest getup I could afford to assemble. (Random but related aside lifted verbatim from funny author Kelly

Oxford's twitter feed recently: "Madonna is older than Blanche was on the first three seasons of *The Golden Girls*." *Think about that, people.*) I paid good money to see the Indigo Girls and Toad the Wet Sprocket before anyone else I knew had even heard of either of them. The problem is, the two CDs I bought at those shows—along with *Like a Virgin*, of course, because it's a classic—are still in my regular rotation.

Yes, I said CDs. I still have hundreds of them, which I listen to inside what was once a badass six-changer Pioneer CD player. It was my high school graduation present—in 1987. I wish I were making this up.

I realize that the music industry has been revolutionized by nifty inventions like MP3 players (which I am pretty sure are the same thing as iPods, but don't quote me on that) and satellite radio and something confusing involving pirates, but I find all of these things extremely complicated to navigate. Besides, how does one discover new music anyway? Sure, I have Pandora on my iPad, but all of my "stations" are grouped by the bands I already know. You know, like Steve Miller and CCR and the artist formerly known as The Artist Formerly Known as Prince but is apparently back to being just Prince. I like to tell myself that my musical tastes aren't outdated— they're *timeless*. They're a little black dress versus a fringy draping of raw meat; creamy hand-churned butter and not imitation margarine-flavor spray.

Fine, my music library is outdated. But ironically, nothing makes me feel younger than stumbling across a beloved tune from my youth. When Elton John's "Bennie and the Jets,"

Free's "All Right Now," Boston's "Rock and Roll Band," Carly Simon's "You're So Vain," or anything by REO Speedwagon comes on, I am instantly transported to that magical time in my life when I was young and carefree and filled with hopeful optimism about the future and dangerously tan yet somehow still wrinkle free. For a blissful three to five minutes, my greatest care in the world is if I should apply the blue eye shadow or the pink, or whether or not it matters if I wear pajamas to class again. I'm riding in a convertible with a boy I've just met and can't wait to kiss, or I'm dancing on the back of my sofa with a beer in my hand, even though I don't even like beer and won't realize this for another ten years. With the flip of a simple, innocent radio dial, I can be cheering for a football team of boys shorter than I am, crying my eyes out in my teenage bedroom over a crush whose name I can't recall, or having my ass grabbed at my senior prom by a guy who'll turn out to be gay. And no hallucinogenic drugs are involved! It's pretty awesome when you think about it.

It's been proven that music has transportive powers like nothing else (except maybe odor, but it's not like you can buy a sawdust-scented CD and pop it in the car whenever you feel like thinking about your beloved late dad who was a builder and always smelled of freshly cut wood, which I would totally do if I could). Scientists like to use complicated explanations involving the prefrontal cortex and "neural correlates of autobiographical memory," but frankly, I'm not all that interested in *why* certain songs act like mini blasts-from-the-past; I'm just grateful that they do.

Because our music was good, right? And not to sound too old lady here,* but back then music used to mean something. We wept when Neil Young sang about the four Kent State University students killed by National Guard Troops for protesting the U.S. invasion of Cambodia; we fist-pumped when Don McLean crooned about Buddy Holly's death, serial killer Charles Manson, and the Kennedy assassination (all in the same song!). "And while Lenin read a book on Marx, a quartet practiced in the park, and we sang dirges in the dark the day the music died." Makes you feel a little weepy just reading that, doesn't it? Compare those words to, for example, "And I was like baby, baby, baby, oh" or "I don't know what's gotten into me, but I kinda think I know what it is." Not quite the same depth of emotion or political awareness, would you agree? Or take my kids' current favorite song, "Thrift Shop," which is chock-full of poignant lyrical prose like "I, I'm a huntin', looking for a come-up, this is fucking awesome."

(If you haven't heard the tune—because you live under a rock—you have to sing that last line all choppy like, as if you were clapping out the syllables. If it were a tweet, you'd type it like this: *This. Is. Fuck. Ing. Awe. Some.*)

To be clear, my kids listen to the "clean" version of "Thrift Shop," which conveniently bleeps out the f-bomb—among countless other sacrileges that would turn the Swear Jar into a full-ride college scholarship fund if you sang it out loud even a

---

* I'm totally going to sound totally old lady here, but the cool kind of old lady who wears skull tank tops and swears a lot.

handful of times—but they know what that *bleeping* beat stands for, believe me. We actually had a long debate about the whole popping-tag thing, too. Was the artist, Macklemore, planning to covertly snip the price tags off of these incredibly desirable secondhand wares and steal them, I asked my kids? Or would the alleged tag popping occur *after* this nice young man had actually purchased these items,* did they suppose? (My pure-hearted children are convinced that Macklemore would never steal.) And what the hell is a "come-up," anyway? Is it like a comeuppance? Because that's a punishment, Mack, so I'm not sure why you'd be scouring thrift stores for one of those. *Unless you were planning to steal a bunch of shit by popping off the tags!*

[Do it with me: Twist head sadly on neck, and mutter "kids" with despair.]

"My Welcome-to-Midlife Moment Was . . ."

When I brought earplugs to a Sting concert.

—ANNE

Of course, the musical generation gap is fairly infamous, with each subsequent age-group firmly and fully believing that the "best" music was the stuff being written and recorded in

---

* Which in the song includes but isn't limited to a broken keyboard, a skeet blanket—whatever that is—flannel zebra jammies, and a big-ass coat.

their personal youth, and that anything produced after that period is pure garbage. If you could time travel back to my childhood home—yes, the one with orange Formica counters and avocado shag carpeting and depressingly dark wood-paneled walls—you'd hear conversations like this on any given day:

MY PARENTS: Turn down that lousy, stinking, godforsaken noise!

ME: *Whoa, whoa, whoa, whoa, whoa, whoa, whoa, whoa, whoa! We are young!!!*

MY PARENTS: TURN DOWN THAT LOUSY, STINKING, GODFORSAKEN NOISE!

ME: *No one can tell us we're—* Wait, WHAT?

MY PARENTS: TURN. DOWN. THAT. LOUSY. STINKING. GODFORSAKEN. NOISE!!!!!

ME: What are you *talking* about? This is Pat Benatar! She's won like a bazillion Grammys, and she's practically the most amazing musician ever born.

MY PARENTS: Amazing? She looks like a man, and she sounds like a feral barn cat getting an enema. You want to hear some *real* music? Put on that Elvis album over there . . .

ME: Elvis? That's your idea of good music. *Elvis?* He sounds like the teacher in Charlie Brown. Only drunker.

MY PARENTS: *[making the sign of the cross]:* Speak that way about the King again and you can find another place to live.

It turns out, hating your kids' or parents' music may be a biological reality we couldn't escape if we wanted to. Scientists have determined that the years from age ten to twenty-five are our key memory-building years, peaking between sixteen and twenty. Ergo, the songs we hear as teenagers stay at the top of our playlists because they become hardwired into our memory during this critical neurological time. When study subjects are asked to rate their three favorite records, movies, and books, participants overwhelmingly pick music they listened to during that peak period. (Favorite books and movies, on the other hand, are far more likely to have been read or watched recently.)

Want to see this phenomenon in heartwarming action? Pull up a YouTube video (boringly) called "Old Man in Nursing Home Reacts to Hearing Music from His Era." Right before your very eyes, a mostly unresponsive elderly patient practically comes back from the dead when given his favorite old-timey music to listen to. It's quite lovely and uplifting to watch, and the best part is that the effects don't end when the song does. After a musical interlude, you see this normally mute man, one who is otherwise unable to answer simple yes-or-no questions, actually engage in articulate conversation. (Of course, at this point all I'm doing is picturing my daughters in eighty or ninety years having "Thrift Shop" shot via a laser through their corneas and into their brains—or whatever the musical delivery system of the time is—and suddenly bursting out of their wheelchairs and bellowing, "This. Is. Bleep. Ing. Awe. Some!!!!" And then I get really sad that I won't be alive to see it.)

It turns out the whole my-generation's-music-kicks-your-generation's-music's-ass thing is not limited to humans. In fact, interesting studies on mice have found that rodents who had been exposed to certain songs during similarly key developmental phases chose resting places playing that very music when they got older. (Mice in the studies not exposed to any music at all sought silence. Grumpy old mice!) It sounds Orwellian, but the bottom line is that in a way we don't even get to choose the music that we like, but rather it chooses us.

Although he's only six years older than me, my husband was obviously listening to a very different radio station than I was during that peak formative period. To say our musical tastes occasionally clash is like saying rats and rattlesnakes sometimes have trouble cuddling. The first few years of our marriage we'd have some variation of this conversation whenever he was responsible for choosing the music:

ME: Who *is* this?

HUSBAND: Guess Who.

ME: Um, a bunch of dead guys I'd rather not be listening to?

HUSBAND: No, Guess Who.

ME: I just did. I give up.

HUSBAND: That's the band's name, Jenna. The Guess Who.

ME: Well, that's the stupidest name I've ever heard, so I'm putting in ABBA.

HUSBAND: Oh God, not ABBA. Please, anything but ABBA. How about Led Zeppelin? Black Sabbath? Genesis?

ME: Blondie?

HUSBAND: The Who?

ME: Blondie. You know, Debbie Harry? Of the band
Blondie?

HUSBAND: I know who Blondie is, I was suggesting
the Who.

ME: Who? You cannot be serious.

Eventually we figured out that we both like Foreigner,
Queen, ELO, and Kiss,* so we didn't have to get divorced. But
when we're mad at each other, it's often a race to see who can
get to Pandora first and put on the other's most-hated music.
Because we're really mature like that.

" My Welcome-to-Midlife Moment Was . . . "

When I had to Google "twerking" . . . DON'T DO IT!

—CRYSTAL

Thanks to having "tweenage" daughters, I'm at least familiar with that music scene. I've seen the Justin Bieber, Hannah Montana, and Katy Perry movies (and yes, I cried like a
little bitch watching all three of them), and I can confidently
identify which one is Demi Lovato and which one is Selena

---

* Actually the only Kiss song I really like is "Beth," because goddamnit
that's a great song.

Gomez. I know every lyric to every Taylor Swift song ever written, even though I can't help but silently mock the twenty-three-year-old's appalling lack of perspective when she croons wistfully about "feeling twenty-two." (Damn it! I should have titled this book *I Don't Know about You but I'm Feeling Forty-Four.*) This isn't always a good thing, of course. I've been busted at the gym singing along with One Direction, and once when Joe and I were driving to L.A. without the kids, we realized halfway there that we'd been listening to our daughters' Disney Jams 15 CD on a continual loop. And singing along with it. But just the other day, the girls came home from school with a magical surprise in store for me.

"Just a small-town squirrel," my youngest began singing. Of course I recognized the tune immediately.

"It's *girl*," I corrected her. She ignored me.

"Living in a lovely world," her sister joined in.

"It's *lonely*," I shouted. "*Lonely* world!"

They kept singing.

"How do you guys know this song?" I asked, astounded.

"We learned it in music class," they informed me. "It's awesome! We love it!"

I started the next line for them. Now it was their turn to look surprised.

"How do you know this song?" they demanded, with insulting emphasis on the *you*, I might add.

"This song was one of my favorites when I was your age," I told them, all nostalgic.

They exchanged glances, clearly debating whether or not

they could continue to like the tune given this new information. Finally, they caved.

"Born and raised in self-control!" they shouted.

"It's South Detroit," I interjected.

"What?" they asked this time, exasperated and annoyed at being interrupted again.

"That line," I explained, thinking to myself *holy shit I totally used to think it was self-control!* "It's not 'born and raised in self-control,' it's 'born and raised in *South Detroit*.' Detroit is a city in Michigan."

"Whatever," they said. "Born and raised in *self-control*! He took the midnight train going *a-ny-where!!!!!!*"

I swear, this happened. My music was their music and it was all kinds of awesome. Whatever you do, don't stop believing, you guys.

CHAPTER 16

Wait, Why Did I Come in Here Again?

Remember that movie *Groundhog Day*? In case you've forgotten the plot—*not because you're old*, but because who can remember a movie that came out before wireless Internet even existed?—it's the one where Bill Murray plays egomaniacal meteorologist Phil Connors. In the film, Phil is not at all happy about having to cover the local Groundhog Day festivities for the fourth miserable year in a row. Perhaps because he's being such an ass about the whole thing, Phil unwittingly finds himself living in some gruesome time warp where *every goddamned day* is Groundhog Day.

I know how Phil feels. But instead of having to report on the actions of a "weather forecasting rat" as Phil calls his furry nemesis, my version of eternally looping-hell looks like this:

Picture me, standing in my pantry—or in my bathroom or the garage or one of the girls' bedrooms or my office—looking around pleadingly, searchingly, desperate to remember why the hell I came in there in the first place.

"Mom!" my daughters will shout, because obviously the minute I step out of their immediate line of vision, especially if it's to use the bathroom, they desperately need me.

"Shhh!" I shout back. "I'm *thinking*." Was I looking for toilet paper? Lightbulbs? Coffee filters? Cat litter? Did I come in to collect dirty laundry? Put clean laundry away? Clip my toenails? Brush my teeth? Remove a splinter? Get new batteries for the remote? Organize eleven years of photos into albums? Clean up dog puke? *And how can I not know this?* For the record, it's not like my house is palatial or anything. How is it that a person can march very purposely the brief distance from Point A to Point B—probably banging her thigh into the corner of the sofa table in her rush to get there—and not remember a mere seven seconds later what that Very Important Purpose was?

You can't imagine how relieved I was when I read a recent headline in *Time* magazine heralding this bit of excellent news: "The Boundary Effect: Entering a New Room Makes You Forget Things." I dug into the article, fascinated and expectant. Apparently, researchers at Notre Dame took it upon themselves to study the widespread phenomenon—it was a widespread phenomenon!—of getting where you're going only to realize you have no idea why you're there. It turns out the culprit is in the construction. The researchers theorize that the simple act of passing through a doorway serves as an "event boundary" in the mind, effectively shutting off what happened in one room and filing any related info away to open space for exciting new things to happen in the next. You know, like clipping your toenails or unearthing the Charmin Ultra. Recalling the decision to do something in the first room is next to impossible, the scientists explain, because that information has already been neatly stowed away. In other words, if I lived in giant loft, I wouldn't even be writing about this, and furthermore, I am not old and forgetful;* I'm just *exceptionally efficient at mental organization*. Obviously.

Anyway, at the end of the *Time* article, the author offers several (okay, two) helpful suggestions for breaking through these frustrating event boundaries:

Mentally repeat your intention as you enter a room/ announce what you're about to do. ("I'm going to get mustard, I'm going to get mustard, QUIT TALKING TO ME GODDAMMIT *GOING TO GET MUSTARD* NO YOU CANNOT WATCH TV *GETTING MUSTARD* I TOLD YOU TO CLEAN YOUR ROOMS *ON MY WAY TO GET MUSTARD* AND WHO LET THE DOG IN HERE *GETTING MUSTARD GETTING MUSTARD GETTING MUSTARD* . . . ")

Move to a one-room apartment.

---

* Incidentally, the article never once called the Boundary Effect a "widespread *middle-age* phenomenon," but have you ever once seen your kids do this? Me neither.

I am not making this up. But still, it makes me feel infinitely better when I'm standing in the pantry/office/garage scanning the space in frustration to know that it's *all the goddamned doorway's fault.*

It's not just the why-am-I-in-here episodes that concern me (although since those occur almost daily, they're by far the most annoying). I find myself forgetting things all the time lately—things I'm famous for *not* forgetting, like birthdays and dentist appointments and conference calls. I even showed up at the gynecologist on the wrong day not long ago—a full week before my scheduled appointment. (You want to feel like a total loser? Go ahead and beg another woman, "Listen, do you think maybe you could just take a quick peek down there since I showered and shaved and paid for parking and everything?") I've left my kids' completed homework packets on planes, permanently misplaced two beach chairs—did I just pack the rest of my shit up, shake out my towel, and walk away? I have no idea!—and honestly, if looking for one's car keys were a book, mine would be called *Where the Fuck Is That Wily Sonofabitch Waldo Now?*

> ## " My Welcome-to-Midlife Moment Was . . . "
>
> When I said to my daughter recently, "Oh, honey, you know I can't read that without my glasses." What made it worse is that then I asked, "Can you find them for me?" and they were on top of my head. Shoot me.
>
> **—MARY**

Here's a good example: I like to think of myself and my husband as two of the most ~~anal-retentive~~ organized people I know. Well, just last week we went on a nice little wine country vacation. When we packed up to come home, Joe and I did what we always do: We took turns doing "sweeps" of every room, each invariably finding something the other had missed on the previous sweep—a phone charger still plugged in behind an end table, a single stray sock that had rolled beneath the bed. After seven or eight rounds of this, we felt confident that we had everything we'd come with and locked the door behind us. Turns out we both repeatedly failed to notice my one-hundred-dollar Sonicare toothbrush standing guard by the sink as well as my husband's *entire garment bag* (stuffed with four button-down shirts, an expensive dinner jacket, and his nicest pair of dress shoes) hanging in the otherwise empty closet. It's no wonder we have next to nothing saved for retirement.

My mom and her friends, who are even further along the downward slope than Joe and me, are always joking about "senior moments" and "old-timers disease." Was this the beginning, I began to wonder? I looked up the warning signs of Alzheimer's and immediately wished I hadn't.

Number 1: Memory loss. This includes but isn't limited to forgetting recently learned information, failing to recall important dates or events, and asking for the same information over and over. Just last month I made a huge production about making sure my youngest daughter had all of her things together for her after-school chess class. I reminded her three times that she had chess that day and that I'd be picking her up at the different time/place. Twenty minutes after the normal school dismissal time, I got a call from my friend Hannah. "Um, I just found Sasha wandering around campus. She said she was looking for her chess class . . . but chess is tomorrow." *[Dusts off spot on mantel for Mother of the Year trophy.]*

Number 2: Confusion with time or place. *See previous illustrative story.*

Number 3: Trouble with spatial relationships. *In my defense, I've been a klutz all my life. Surely, I wasn't born with Alzheimer's.*

Number 4: Misplacing things. *Well, fuck.*

Number 5: Decreased or poor judgment. *Do you think wearing my nightie to drop the girls off at school counts if I didn't even get out of the car and wasn't drunk or hungover?*

I am not making fun of a tragic and debilitating disease, I swear. I genuinely am concerned about the fact that I'm not as sharp as I once was. I know from previous research that some scientists theorize that one way to prevent cerebral atrophy is by engaging in mental exercises to enhance brain performance. The idea being that because most of us spend our days performing primarily routine, unconscious actions—brushing our teeth, driving the same route to work, cooking the same meals, yelling at our kids, and having sex in the exact same position—that we're not exposed to enough sensory stimulation to continue to build new brain cells. By mixing things up, for instance eating with our nondominant hand, getting dressed with our eyes closed, turning the clock upside down and trying to figure out what-the-fuck time it is, mapping a brand-new route to Starbucks, or spinning in a sex hammock clad in only a pair of pasties and a smile, we stimulate our brains to build new dendrites and neurons,* and hopefully, we prevent or at least postpone age-related dementia. It's all good in theory, but still, I highly doubt that I'll become a regular at the brain gym anytime soon. I mean, they probably don't even have a café *or* a boutique, which are the two most motivating reasons to go to any gym, in my opinion.

Wait, what was I talking about?

Oh yeah, forgetting shit.

Obviously, in addition to the "natural decline in cognitive functioning associated with age," part of the problem is that like you, I have approximately 4,593,291 things to remember at any given moment: our daughters' constantly changing extracurricular activities, my approximate checking account balance, things we need at one of the five grocery stores I visit regularly but haven't had time to put on the respective lists, exactly how many waffles we have in the freezer (because you would not believe the shitstorm that went down that one time we ran completely out), my last period, my next mammogram, where I left my checkbook, eleventeen billion passwords to all of the websites I frequent, the names of all of the kids in both of my children's classes *and* their parents, and the perfectly

---

* These are Very Important Brain Parts, and I have no idea what they do because I'm not a doctor or anything. I suggest the Internet if you're curious.

timed lyrics to "Roxanne" so I can kill it on Rock Band, to name just a few. That shit takes up so much mental energy it's a wonder I can rattle off the days of the week with anything resembling accuracy anymore. So when I call my sister and she gets mad at me because *she's at work and didn't I remember that she changed her schedule and now she works Thursday afternoons instead of mornings*, I can get a little defensive.

"I can't recall where I left my yoga mat, I just mailed Mom's birthday present seven weeks late, and my cats haven't had their shots in three years," I tell her. "So no, I can't possibly remember your ever-changing work schedule. But I love you!"

("But I love you!" is how we follow up anything remotely resembling an insult in our family. It's the equivalent of adding a smiley face after a nasty comment in an email. "You look like you haven't slept in a week. But I love you! ☺" See how that softens the blow?)

True story: One recent morning I was idling about the kitchen, taking my sweet time packing the girls' lunches, when my youngest padded into the kitchen.

"Mom, did you forget about chorus?" she asked.

Two mornings a week for the past eight months I'd been waking her an hour early so she could participate in the school's chorus practice. Not only that, but when she started, I had joined a workout group with a bunch of my friends who had kids in chorus, too, so everyone was already up and out at the same ridiculously early hour anyway. Because of this, chorus was something I knew I'd never forget.

Except I did. I totally forgot. It wasn't that I had my days mixed up, either, because the whole what-day-is-it-and-what-do-we-have routine never even crossed my mind.

"Oh my gosh, what's wrong with me?" I said, mostly rhetorically, shuffling into high speed so that she'd at least make the last half of practice and I could squeeze in a few push-ups.

"Nothing," my ever-sweet daughter replied, wrapping her arms around my middle. "You're just old!"

It's too bad brain space isn't like a closet you can just go through periodically and purge of the stuff you don't need anymore. Because seriously, I have some wildly useless bits of trivia floating around upstairs that refuse to acknowledge that they are obsolete. I can list every teacher I've ever had beginning in preschool and continuing through college (a feat I didn't even realize was unusual until my husband said he could probably name two, tops). The dog on *The Jetsons*? Astro. The cat on *The Brady Bunch*? Fluffy. (The dog was Tiger, if you're wondering.) The intercom guy you never saw on *Rhoda*? Carlton Your Doorman, of course. The quadratic formula, the Pythagorean theorem, and an alphabetical list of the world's English prepositions (aboard, about, above, across, after, against, along, amid, among . . .): these are all things I can reel off *without Google's help*. I also still know my first grade best friend's phone number, every word to "Miss Lucy Had a Tugboat," and exactly what I was wearing in 1979 the first time I flew on a plane by myself.* Would you care to hear the

---

* White parachute pants with a different colored zipper on every pocket and at the ankles with a matching jacket, because I know you're dying to know.

entire "Is this a dagger which I see before me" *Macbeth* so-liloquy I recited in tenth grade or the reading from the Letter of Paul to the Philippians I delivered during a Parent's Day mass in third grade? Not a problem, pull up a seat and get comfy. With all of this crap crammed into my mental filing cabinet—which surely has only a finite amount of space—it's no wonder I can't recall the name of the guy I was introduced to fifteen seconds ago and have to use my car remote's panic button to find the thing in the Rite Aid parking lot more often than not.

Sometimes I (secretly) blame my children for my dwin-dling wits and forehead creases, but if a recent bee study turns out to apply to humans as well, the scary reality is that I'd be even dumber and more haggard-looking without them. Sci-entists have discovered that when mama bees remain in their nests and take care of their babies, their mental competence stays more or less the same. But when they leave the nest to gather food, aging accelerates faster than a seventeen-year-old kid chasing a car full of naked hookers on the Autobahn. After just two weeks, the researchers found, bees that left their little ones behind have worn wings, hairless bodies, and sig-nificantly reduced brain functioning, specifically measured as the ability to learn new things. (Sound familiar?) But check this out: When the mama bees are forced out of foraging mode and sent back to care for their babies, their brainpower skyrockets once again. And as it happens, the proteins that the big-brained bees produce when they're on nest duty are the very same ones humans produce.

I think the lesson here is that while you can't blame your children for your forgetfulness,* there are still great benefits to having them. For instance, tomorrow when you're cuddling on the couch watching *America's Funniest Home Videos* with them and feeling guilty because you're not doing anything "productive," you can tell yourself that you're doing it for your brain. (Just don't tell your husband this. He'll insist the benefit is all in the TV-watching, and you'll never, ever get him to mow the lawn again.)

---

* Although if they'd never been born, you'd probably never forget to pick them up from school, I'm just saying.

CHAPTER 17

....

Abject Poverty, Bunny Boilers, and Other Reasons I Will Never Have an Affair

Even though I have no plans to engage in any of the many characteristic activities associated with the proverbial "midlife crisis," I'll admit I can understand at least some of them. As I've mentioned, I'd get a face-lift and a sexy new car ~~tomorrow~~ this afternoon if money and risk of death weren't two very real, prohibiting factors. And even though I don't have my own laminated list of Things I Want to Do before I Die, I respect and appreciate the effort and enthusiasm that goes into crafting such an ambitious registry. But the one thing I cannot— and never will—fathom is the midlife extramarital affair.

Don't get me wrong. I suppose it's possible to imagine what might motivate *other people who didn't get as lucky as I did in the spousal department and, therefore, aren't as blissfully happy* *as I am* to entertain the idea of a fling in the fantasy realm. And of course I've wondered what it might be like to experience a delicious stretch of unfamiliar flesh beneath my fingers or to feel the sweet flutter of butterfly wings in my belly again when an unknown pair of lips brushes the back of my neck.* I also get how it's tempting to think that all of my other miserable worries would melt away if I were simply being worshiped as a beautiful and interesting goddess for even a half hour every other week. And who couldn't use a good kick in the ass to get into bikini shape? But I also believe in integrity and honesty and being true to your word, and I very distinctly recall promising that I would be faithful to one man and one man only *until death did us part* (even though as I pointed out in my last book, it's hard to comprehend exactly how long that can feel until you're knee-deep in it). So as long as Joe and I have even a weak pair of pulses between us, and he hasn't done something unforgivingly egregious like hit me or sign a billion-year contract pledging his loyalty to a religion that worships the alien ruler of the Galactic Federacy who came to earth seventy-five million years ago in a spaceship,† or have an affair of his own, I'm in this for the long haul. Besides—and I don't think I can put too fine a point on this, really—who the hell has time for all that a steamy extramarital affair would entail?

I'll be honest, it's hard enough for me to carve a big enough

---

* I wondered it one time, honey, and we were in a *huge* fight.

† I'm sorry but Scientology is a total deal breaker for me.

sliver out of my schedule for a handful of shags a month with *one* guy (and believe me, it's not like we're Sting and Trudie over here). And the one I've got now happens not to care if I shave my legs or brush my teeth first! Ostensibly, if I were getting some side action as well and hoping not to get caught, I'd have to maintain my wifely duties at home while also finding twenty or thirty extra hours each week to groom, send hundreds of titillating sext messages, sculpt sexy abs, conspire about possible rendezvous locations, obsess about every inch of my naked body, hide mountains of evidence, fabricate fake appointments, bribe friends to be reliable and convincing alibis, panic about being caught, and then actually have sex with this person.

I get exhausted just thinking about it.

Besides, my husband and I both work from home, so how on earth would I pull it off?

"Bye, honey!" I'd try to trill casually, mentally calculating the fastest route to the Motel 6.

"Where're you going?" Joe would ask innocently, reflexively, because *we always ask each other this* when one or the other actually leaves the house—which isn't often.

"Oh, to the grocery store," I'd mutter, thinking to myself, *Christ now I have to come home with groceries! I hope Xander is naked and ready to go when I get there.*

"Are you wearing . . . *eye makeup*?" Joe would demand, stepping in closely to inspect my unusually plump lashes.

"Oh yeah, maybe a little mascara," I'd stammer, rubbing my nose— Shit, that's the first sign you're supposed to look for to see if someone is lying! Did he read that issue of *Psychology Today*, too?—and patting my bangs down over my eyes. "I, um . . . I got a free sample, so I was trying it out."

Oh, what a tangled web we weave . . .

"You smell really nice, too," he'd say, sniffing around my neck and starting to sound accusing.

"New deodorant," I'd mutter, brushing past him with a peck on the cheek.

When first we practice to deceive . . .

"What time will you be back?" he'd call to my back.

"Couple hours," I'd reply vaguely. "I need to hit the bank, too, and the shoe repair place, and then I have to pick up some tampons and stop by the gynecologist to drop off an endometrial tissue sample . . ."

(The tampon and gynecologist stuff is something an older, wiser colleague taught me at my very first job. "If you ever need to skip out for a personal errand or want to go to the gym," my astute new friend had advised me, "just mumble something vague involving feminine hygiene, and nobody will ask any questions." I'm sure that our boss thought I had herpes or cervical dysplasia or at least some benign fibroid tumors for the amount of time I supposedly spent dealing with my troubled lady parts.)

If you think this is an exaggeration, I promise you that just a few weeks ago my husband became inordinately suspicious when he came up to my office to find me in a bathrobe with a towel wrapped around my wet hair.

"You going somewhere?" he asked.

"Nope," I told him, typing away.

"Well, how come you took a shower?" he wanted to know.

"I do that every once in a while," I reminded him.

"Yeah, but in the middle of the day?" he demanded.

"Fine," I said. "I'm having an affair." And then we laughed and laughed about the fact that *taking a lousy shower* was cause for questioning around here. Can you imagine if I were shaving my legs more than twice a month?

As if the lying and vow breaking and finding time for illicit activities parts of hypothetically cheating on my husband weren't enough of a deterrent, after thirteen years of Catholic schooling I'm pretty sure the guilt would kill me. Hell, I feel bad when I swaddle my leftovers in misleading wrapping and bury them in the back of the fridge so Joe won't find and eat them. Plus I read once that having an affair breaks *six* of the Ten Commandments—and actually more if you hook up with your fling on the holy Sabbath or accidentally cry out "Oh my God" during sex. Risking eternal damnation in Hades's fiery pit with all of the other souls of the damned just doesn't seem worth it for a few rounds of hide-the-salami, even if it *is* a really delicious and exotic piece of meat unlike anything you have in your refrigerator at home.

Also? Surely, I can't be the only person who was totally and permanently traumatized by the movie *Fatal Attraction*. That flick came out the year I graduated from high school, and my guess is that if you looked at a longitudinal graph of extramarital activity throughout the century, there'd be a titanic dip right there at the 1987 mark. There's nothing like watching a seemingly normal woman seduce a married man with electric elevator sex and then immediately embark on a psycho murderous rampage to convince you that infidelity can be risky. That crazy bitch *cooked* his kid's pet bunny! For the love of all that is furry, that's just . . . *wrong*. Well done, Hollywood. Well done.*

Let's not forget that one of the greatest benefits of being married is not having to date anymore or pretend to be captivated by another person's interests or tiresome life history. It's been nearly two decades since I've had to do this, and I honestly don't think I could muster even two ounces of fake enthusiasm. "So, what was your childhood like? How many brothers and sisters do you have? What are your thoughts on life after death?" *Now I'm going to have to remember all of this crap? Where exactly am I going to store this information?* Not to mention at some point I'd likely be expected to share all of my own personal baggage again—which, honestly, is not something that anybody I'm not paying $150 an hour should ever have to hear. And I don't know about you, but I'd eat pickled rattlesnake meat doused in kerosene if it meant I never again had to back away from the bed in what I'm praying is a seductive manner so that the guy in it wouldn't catch a glimpse of my flabby, dimpled ass.

Of course no anti-affair argument would be complete without a section on the potential financial consequences. Suppose I'm

---

* Not at all a reference to how rabbit meat should be cooked.

considering an affair right at this very minute. For argument's sake, let's assume the hypothetical object of my illicit affection is not in fact a Saudi sheikh, retired anesthesiologist, or Warren Buffet. This means that I'm going to have to find a way to pony up for my share of the hotel rooms, plane tickets, sexy lingerie, personal training sessions, romantic dinners, condoms, and whipped cream we'll be needing. Of course, all of this will have to be paid for in cash so that there's no pesky paper trail for my unsuspecting husband to find and follow. Two measly trysts a month could easily add up to a cool grand, and the chances of me squirreling away that much cash unnoticed are up there with Chelsea Handler's odds of becoming a nun.

Even if my boy toy is fabulously flush and willing to foot the entire bill for our extracurricular activities, surely I'll still want a few new pairs of Hanky Pankys and the occasional spray tan—neither of which could be purchased with the spare change hiding beneath my couch cushions. I cringe at the thought of having to be all, "Um, Mohammad Ali-Algebra? Do you think you could spot me fifty bucks so I can pick up some panties that have actual working elastic? I promise I'll make it worth your while [wink wink]."

Then let's imagine for a minute that Mohammad and I get a little sloppy—he forgets his turban after a quickie in the backseat of my SUV, or one of his eleven wives walks in on us enjoying a nice Jacuzzi bath and snaps a scandalous iPhone photo that she promptly forwards to the local newspaper—do you think my honorable, blameless husband is going to let me off the hook easily?

Oh no. No, he is not.

And when he kicks my ass to the curb, where exactly am I going to go? How am I going to come up with the first month's rent, last month's rent, and security deposit on my shitty ghetto apartment? (You know as well as I do that Mohammad dropped me like a steaming diaper the minute our hot tub photo hit the front page under the headline "Wealthy Sheikh Caught Slumming with Middle-Aged Soccer Mom.") Even if I somehow manage to put a feeble roof over my sad, pathetic head, how am I possibly going to pay for little luxuries like a bed and a shower curtain and food to put in my ancient, rusty refrigerator? You think I'm getting alimony? Please. I wasn't smart enough to sit back and pop bonbons and watch soap operas all day and let my husband support me during our marriage, so he will be under no obligation to finance me now.

"God damn you, Mohammad!" I weep into my dirty pillowcase. (My apartment didn't come with a washer and dryer, and have you been to a Laundromat lately? Dis*gusting*.) "You said you loved me! And I believed you. And Joe! Sweet, loyal, dependable Joe. How could I do this to you? To our family? To *us*? God, I'm an idiot. A total, fucking, absolute, penniless idiot!"

Oh yeah, our family. Nice example I'm setting for my daughters over here, right?

"But Mommy, you *lied*," they'd cry, confused and disappointed.

"Yes, yes, I did," I'd have to confess.

"You said that lying was the worst thing we could ever do,"

they'd say between gasping sobs as they watched me pack my suitcase.

"I sure did," I'd agree, taking out some shoes to make room for the Vitamix blender, because I love my green smoothies and that machine costs four hundred dollars and where am I going to get that kind of money now?

"But how come it was okay for *you* to lie, then?" they'd want to know.

"Well, honey, there are lots of things I can do that you can't," I'd say, trying to rationalize away their pain and my guilt at the same time. "Like, I can drink margaritas and drive a car and have babies, and you can't, right? You'll understand someday."

"So we get to lie when we're grown-ups?" they'll ask, suddenly all giddy.

"Sure you can!" I'd have to tell them. "Just make sure you're totally positive you can get away with it—and that you can afford to support yourself if you get caught."

Despite the tremendous disaster potential inherent in cheating on your spouse, married people have affairs every day. If you're not lucky enough to be seduced by a dude at work or lock eyes with the lust of your life while you're waiting for your foot fungus prescription to be filled at Costco, you can always hop on over to one of the many websites like AshleyMadison .com (tagline: "Life is short. Have an affair.") that have been specifically created to help married cheaters hook up with other married cheaters. *Oh, people don't really do that,* you say, shaking your head in disbelief. Really? I guess those 1,800,000 unique visitors every single month land there by looking for stories about Ashley Olsen strolling down Madison Avenue, or searching for cute names should they find out they're pregnant with twin girls. What? It could happen.

Pick up any random issue of *People* magazine at your nail salon, and you'll find proof of a simple fact: Affairs make people crazy. They crush reputations, alienate friends, and ruin lives. Tiger Woods lost his stunning supermodel wife (not to mention the 750 million bucks he had to turn over to her, plus high-profile endorsement deals with Accenture, AT&T, Gatorade, GM, and TAG Heuer, resulting in combined shareholder losses estimated to be between five and twelve billion dollars—yes, *billion* with a *B*) because he couldn't keep his pants zipped around porn stars. Jude Law cheated on lovely Sienna Miller with the fucking *babysitter*, which I am pretty sure is every wife's worst nightmare and hopefully will come back like a giant karmic boomerang to smack him in the ass in a big and painful way someday. Bill Clinton risked the *Presidency of the United States* for a blowjob from a chubby White House intern. Clearly, seeing as how by most scientific accounts humans aren't even meant to be monogamous in the first place, a little side action is tough to resist.

Of course it's not always the famous fellows who are the philanderers: LeAnn Rimes, Tori Spelling, Heidi Klum, J-Lo, Madonna, Kristen Stewart, Whoopi Goldberg, Meg Ryan, Elizabeth Taylor, Jessica Simpson, Anne Heche, Britney Spears, Kate Hudson, and Princess Diana—may her royal soul rest in peace—are all reportedly card-carrying members of the Lying,

Cheating, Home-Wrecking Whores Club. And for what? A different set of hands grabbing your ass while you brush your teeth, or a new brand of stinky basketball socks on top of your hamper lid? No thanks. I think I'll stick with the lovably bumbling oaf I've already got.

·····················

CHAPTER 18

But I Lived in the
Moment Yesterday

Another under-recognized hallmark of this magical midlife period (besides owning Muffin Top Stoppers and having totally frozen foreheads and pinning bucket lists to our virtual bulletin boards, of course) would have to be a fascination with new age crap.

From tai chi to feng shui, everyone's doing it, at least in my social circles. Friendships born of bar dancing and party hopping now involve more navel gazing and soul searching than I'd care to admit. We read books about Ayurveda together and contemplate the colors of our auras—mine is green, apparently, which suggests I'm powerful, organized, and intelligent, so obviously auras are both existent and accurate—and help each other rid our new homes of bitter old spirits by parading about

·············

the properties with burning stalks of sage. (We really do this.) We've traded step aerobics for hot Vinyasa classes (performed in one-hundred-degree rooms to "maximize detoxification and intensity," not to mention "maximize the nasal assault of compounded bodily odors caused by practicing yoga in overcrowded one-hundred-degree rooms") and covered our LA VIDA LOCA tattoos with much more demure and tasteful third-eye designs. We download meditation challenges to our iPods, and then *we actually do them*. And some of us—not me, I swear—spend our precious vacation time and money at new age spas doing asinine things like having strangers rhythmically tap wooden pegs into our backs with a tiny hammer and shove hoses up our assholes.* Oh yes, we are the crystal-clutching hippies my conservative blue-collar parents warned me about.

It started gradually, of course. One day Carrie casually mentioned an upcoming trip to a holistic spa. Pam asked if she could borrow my copy of *The Power of Now* ("Shelly has it, ask her to give it to you when she's done."). Formerly normal conversations were suddenly peppered with stories about *emerging* this and *manifesting* that and *invoking* God knows what, but still I didn't think much of it. After all, I live in Southern California, which last time I checked was a notorious granola gathering spot. But then a New York friend—a high-powered finance guy, mind you—went on a "spiritual trek" to India and a pal from London gave up marathon running for tai chi

---

* I'm referring, of course, to Manaka Tapping Treatments and colonic irrigation, respectively.

and one of my best friends in South Carolina started raving about how Transcendental Meditation (TM to devotees) was *changing her life*, and I realized it had nothing to do with zip codes.

(Aside: In case you're not familiar with TM—and I wasn't, either—according to Wikipedia,* it's a specific type of "self-development mantra meditation," which costs thousands of dollars to learn and "has been incorporated into selected schools, universities, corporations, and prison programs in the USA." And you *know* it's got to be awesome if they're using it on inmates and you can't pick it up by watching a YouTube video, right?)

I've given this some thought, and I think it's legit to liken the midlife interest in spiritual enlightenment to hiking: When you're climbing *up* the mountain, you're only thinking about the top—how great you'll feel when you get there and how beautiful the view will be and how nice it will be to finally sit down and how delicious that PowerBar in your back pocket is going to taste if you remember to take it out before you sit down. But when you start the downhill descent and you're no longer focused on the effort or the payoff, your thoughts turn to the more distant future: the bath you'll have to give the tick-covered dog when you get home and what's for dinner and basically all of the other crap you have to look forward to after your hike.

---

* Which is the definitive last word on pretty much everything, obviously.

Just yesterday-ish we were too busy husband hunting and baby making and/or clawing our collective way up countless corporate ladders to give a rat's ass about the purpose, the point of it all. Now suddenly, we're all holding mudras and chanting mantras and standing in public parks on one foot, all crazy Mr. Miyagi style, and trying our best to "be still and go within," whatever the hell that means. "It's all about the mind-body connection," our gurus tell us, which seems a little redundant to me because one without the other is either a transplant waiting to happen or a zucchini.

On the surface I am one of the enlightenment seekers, but I have to admit I'm sort of half-assed about it. I do have a vision board, but the contents rarely change, and I still don't have an infinity pool or a Range Rover, so obviously, I'm not doing it right, but I haven't bothered to figure out how or why. I only buy milk and eggs from happy cows and chickens that are able to roam freely when they're not producing my breakfast staples, but I also eat crap way more than I should.* I bought my own copy of *The Secret* DVD as soon as it came out, and I have every intention of watching it one of these years. I believe that thoughts have energy, yet I still carry around plenty of shitty ones. I did try to get my chakras cleaned, you may recall, but

---

* True story: On my daughter's tenth birthday I asked her what she wanted for her special dinner and she replied hopefully, "Can we *please* have crap mac and cheese? Everyone else gets it all the time, and I've never even had it!"
"Do you mean *Kraft* mac and cheese?" I asked. *[Confused look.]*

I was only willing to invest a measly five bucks in gleaming energy centers, so what does that tell you?

It was a trip to a regular old Western medicine doctor that convinced me I had some work to do.

"Are you tired a lot?" the Harvard-trained professional asked after the routine exam.

"Oh my God, *exhausted*, constantly," I told her.

"Do you get irritated easily?" she wanted to know.

"Um, some people might say that . . ." I admitted, thinking she was about to tell me I was officially menopausal.

"You've got muscle and joint pain, and your blood pressure is about as low as it can be and still allow basic functioning," she continued.

"I agree, I'm a wreck," I told her. "So what do I need? Surgery? Vitamins? A complete overhaul?"

"You need to relax," she said simply. *You think?*

"I'm pretty sure you told me that last year," I replied.

"And I'm pretty sure you didn't do it," she countered. "You have no balance. You go, go, go all day long, and your adrenal glands are shot. You need to rejuvenate yourself. Have you tried yoga or meditation?" This wasn't some alterna–witch doctor doling out this advice; this was my primary care physician, one who accepted real insurance and everything.

"I can't meditate, and yoga is boring," I told her. "It's so . . . *still*."

"Yes, you can—if you want to—and the stillness is the point," she insisted.

I paid my co-pay and left, swinging by Starbucks on the

way home because *man was I tired after all of that poking and prodding and exhausting talk about yoga.*

I managed to put the whole chat out of my mind for a while. But recently, when I started feeling even more run-down and irritable and achy than usual, I started thinking seriously about what she had said. I really have tried meditating, but honestly, my thoughts are like a room full of sugared-up kindergarteners in a bounce house: good luck trying to quiet them. I've also done plenty of yoga in my life, and while I like the physicality of it, I have no patience for the esoteric mumbo jumbo part. (*That's the point,* my doctor whispers in my ear. I mentally poke her in the third eye.)

On the other hand, Madonna does yoga, and she's *fifty-five* with the body of someone half her age. I suppose if I'm going to take any steps toward inner peace and tranquility, I might as well get buff arms out of the deal. My mind made up, I buy myself some cute yoga pants and a cushy mat and a month of unlimited classes at a local studio for less than I'd pay for a few venti lattes,* excited to watch my life be transformed.

I will be disciplined and dedicated and totally . . . yogic, I tell myself. Yogic! That's actually a word. I feel smug just thinking it.

On my first day of class, the sinewy yoga instructor strides into the studio. "Namaste, I'm Summer," she says with a languid bow by way of introduction. *Of course you are. I guess that makes me Fall.* (What? Old habits die hard.) "Let's start today

---

* Seriously, how awesome is Groupon?

by standing with our feet firmly rooted in the earth, closing our eyes, and opening our hearts."

I try not to roll my eyes. I am pretty sure I can stand relatively still, and I probably can even do it with my eyes closed, but I'm a little concerned about the opening my heart bit. Isn't that something best left to skilled cardiac surgeons? *Focus, Jenna. Just focus. Sarcasm is not even a little bit yogic.*

After Summer warms us up with lots of panting, we move into downward-facing dog. I love this pose because my dog does it all the time, and every time he does, I scream, "DOWNWARD-FACING DOG," in the hopes that he'll eventually learn to do it on command. He's thirteen and has yet to pick up this skill. "Breathe into the backs of your knees as you press your heels into the earth," Summer instructs without a trace of irony.

Breathe into the backs of my knees? How exactly would one do that? I know the ankle bone is connected to the shin bone and everything, but I'm almost positive there's no direct airway from my lungs to my middle-leg region. Still, I do my best to will oxygen down into my legs, because I am *yogic* and also because I'd really like to look like Summer.

She's folded practically in half, her heels are flat on the ground, and honest to God, she doesn't have an ounce of body fat on her. In fact, it sort of looks like she's wearing her muscles and tendons on the *outside* of her skin. I catch a glimpse of my own midsection down my ballooning shirt, and while I've never actually viewed the underbelly of a nursing cow before, I am pretty sure I know what it looks like now.

"Quiet your mind as you pull your pelvis away from your lower back," Summer intones.

Listen, hottest of all seasons. Both of those things seem fairly impossible to me on their own; pulling them off simultaneously might be a bit advanced for an intermediate yoga class, don't you think?

I make it through the hour, doing my best to stifle a parade of cynical thoughts, and fall asleep in Savasana. Clearly, I have great yogic potential, because Summer *did* ask us to release all thoughts and revel in the profundity of stillness. You can't imagine how profoundly still I am in that corpse pose.

My first month of classes ends and I buy another. Then, because I'm already on Amazon and have to spend ten more bucks to get the free shipping, I order a few yoga DVDs. I even take them with me when I go away for a few days now. Because—and don't tell anybody I said this, especially my smug-faced doctor—I feel better when I do yoga. Stronger, more flexible, less achy, and maybe even a tiny bit more *balanced.*

Have I learned to quiet my thoughts? Not even close. Do I look like Summer? Only in the sense that we both have four limbs and a nose. Will I ever? The odds are up there with Jenna Marbles being invited to speak at the Vatican. But yoga is the closest I get to Zen, so I'll take it. Plus it beats the hell out of colonic irrigation.

CHAPTER 19

I Liked My Kids Better before They Told Me My Ass Jiggles

Let me start here by saying that I love my daughters more than anything else in the world times infinity plus eleven. Raising them is both my life's greatest joy and most rewarding challenge. I would throw myself in front of a spray of bullets, jump into icy, treacherous rapids, or wrestle a congregation of hungry alligators for either of them without a second's pause.* But I have to tell you, when Joe and I decided to start a family—which was not a

---

* That's what a group of gators is called, a congregation. Why each animal has its own troop name is beyond me, but it would make a killer *Jeopardy!* category. ("What is a <u>shrewdness</u> of apes/a <u>wake</u> of buzzards/a <u>coalition</u> of cheetahs/an <u>implausibility</u> of gnus/a <u>charm</u> of hummingbirds/a <u>scourge</u> of mosquitoes/a <u>prickle</u> of porcupines?")

decision we came to easily or simultaneously, I might add—I had *no flipping idea* what I was getting myself into.

First of all, I can recall every last should-we-or-shouldn't-we debate as if it happened yesterday, and I am 100 percent certain that the object in question each and every time was a baby. Were we ready to have a *baby*? Could we afford to have a *baby*? What would we name the *baby*? Who would be the *baby's* primary, default caregiver? Were my boobs big enough to feed a *baby*? Would Joe be the hottest *baby*-daddy we knew? And how exactly did one swaddle a *baby* anyway?

So now I'm over here scratching my head and wondering how on earth I could possibly be responsible for two extremely large, relentlessly chatty, and downright demanding mini-people who roll their eyes at me on a regular basis and want to know why I'm allowed to get massages and pedicures and they're not. ("Because I have a fucking *job*, that's why!")

"I'm sorry, but I signed up for the *baby* plan?" I've tried shouting, but nobody can hear me over the Taylor Swift that's forever blaring in the background.

My sister got married a decade before I did, so her oldest was turning nine the year I was due with my firstborn.

"He's halfway out of the house," she whimpered on his ninth birthday, with actual tears and everything.

"Are you PMSing?" I asked, baffled. (If my sister wasn't a card-carrying teetotaler, I'd have assumed she was drunk.)

"Jenna, you don't understand," she sobbed. "I don't even know where the last nine years went! It's not enough time. I'm not ready for him to leave!"

And I was considered the "dramatic one"? Unbelievable.

"You have him for at least *nine more years!*" I'd countered, because I hadn't yet entered the accelerated time-sucking vortex that is parenting myself. Nine years was a lifetime, an eternity bordering on infinity. *In nine years,* I thought, *I'll be forty-four!* Hahahaha! I could never be forty-four! That was just crazy talk, and my sister was nuts, and that was all there was to it.

" My Welcome-to-Midlife Moment Was . . . "

When my wife reminded me that when I can finally share my favorite film, *Raiders of the Lost Ark*, with my son, it will be over thirty years old.

—JP

When my daughters actually were babies—and in retrospect, so was I—well-intended strangers constantly approached us with the singular purpose of doling out unsolicited and similarly bewildering advice.

"Ah, enjoy these days," they'd say, looking all misty eyed. "They grow up so fast . . . It goes by in a blink."

I'd look down at the milk rings around my boobs and the spit-up dripping down my shoulder and think, *You people are complete morons. Enjoy these days? I can't wait for them to be over. And you think two decades is going to go by in a blink? Yesterday lasted twelve weeks alone! Time is practically standing still over here!* I honestly couldn't even fathom that these tiny, chubby, hairless, flailing bodies I had produced would ever be capable of walking upright, calling me "meaner than the wicked witch if she existed" or begging for a $1,200 drum kit. It just wouldn't compute.

And then I blinked, and here I am. At this writing, the top of my oldest daughter's head comes up to my nose, a fact I still don't quite believe, and as such, I am constantly looking down to see if she's wearing high heels or standing on her sister. (She almost always isn't.) She has crushes on boys, can apply eye shadow better than I can,* and has already figured out that she'll turn sixteen on a Saturday, which means she'll have to wait an extra two endless, torturous days to get her driver's license than she would if her sweetest of all birthdays fell on a weekday. *Her driver's license!* Ridiculous, right? I mean, babies can't drive *cars.*

When you still think you have babies, you are caught wildly unprepared when your double-digit child comes to you and drops the following bomb: "I asked Dad how babies were made, but he said that you'd be mad at him if he told me."

Oh, he did, did he? Nice deflecting, buddy. No really, I got this one. Been looking forward to it for ages, in fact.

"Why don't you tell me what you already know?" I said,

---

* Of course I don't let her out of the house in it! What kind of mother do you think I am? I do, however, let her do my makeup when I'm going out, because why not?

trying to assess how much playground damage I might need to undo first.

"Literally *nothing*," she insisted.

"Do you know what sex is?" I asked her.

She shook her head sadly.

"Okay," I said, taking a deep breath. (It's worth noting here that I never had this conversation with my own mother, ever. In fact, I have vivid memories of sitting on my living room couch one evening reading my Judy Blume book while my mom was cooking dinner. "Mom, what does m-a-s-t-u-r-b-a-" I hadn't even finished spelling the mystery word when she snatched the book from my hand and sent me to my room. *Ooh, it must be something really good,* I remember thinking. Naturally, I started saving my paltry allowance that minute, and as soon as I had enough money for bus fare and a new book, I hauled my ass to the mall and bought myself another copy. *Which I hid under my mattress,* of course, *because trip once you're clumsy; twice you're stupid.* Who needed a mom who was comfortable talking about sex when you had Judy Blume? Which book *was* that, I wondered now? Maybe I could get a copy for my daughter and call it a day. No, wait. We're supposed to do better than our parents did, to learn from their mistakes and right the wrongs of our histories. We're supposed to be able to talk about sex.)

"So all mommies have seeds in their bodies, and daddies have seeds in *their* bodies," I explained. "You need both seeds to make a baby. So after a man and a woman get married and decide they want to have a baby, even though it's really hard and expensive to have a baby and it hurts really badly when you give birth to it, then the two seeds come together to make the baby."

[To self: Nailed it!]

"How do the seeds get together?" she wanted to know.

"Oh, that," I said. "Well, the daddy plants his seed inside the mommy, where it grows until it's ready to be born." *Answer their questions but don't give them more information than they ask for. Damn, I'm so good at this, I might need to take my show on the road! I'll bet other parents would pony up to have someone else have this conversation for them. Not me, of course. I've got this.*

She thought about my seed story for a minute, nodding her head as the information sank in. Maybe I wouldn't even have to say penis and vagina!

"But how does the daddy's seed *get into* the mommy?" she pressed.

Jesus, kid. Have you ever considered a career in law?

It's just a word. You can say it.

"The penis."

Horrified look.

"What *about* the penis?"

"His seed comes out of his penis."

"And goes *where*?"

[To self: You were given this information once, and it did not in fact kill you. She can handle it. Just spit it out and get it over with.]

"The daddy puts his penis inside the mommy's vagina so the two seeds can come together."

She stood there with an honest-to-God-I-might-vomit expression complete with holding-her-gut-and-cringing posture.

"But . . . *why?*" she demanded.

"That's just the way it works," I explained. *For the record, this was not in the parenting books.* "It's kind of a weird system when you think about it, huh?"

She nodded like a bobblehead with ADHD.

"How long does the penis have to stay in there?" she wanted to know.

"Not that long," I told her, because she was starting to look worried and also because it's true.

Afterward I was regaling my friend Cori with the painful details of my inaugural sex chat with my daughter.

"Oh, I tried the whole husband-and-wife thing with Catelyn, too," she said. "But then she got all quiet and finally she said, 'Wait a minute. Aunt Lori has a baby . . . and she's not married.' I was like, 'Yeah, she got a special permit for that, it's really complicated.'"

"You did not!" I screamed, doubled over in happy tears.

"Oh, I did," Cori insisted. "Even as the words were coming out of my mouth, I was like *what on earth am I saying?* The worst part was when Dave came home I had to tell him that if Catelyn asked anything about the not-married baby permit, he was going to need to go along with it."

These conversations, of course, are the beginning of the

end. The end of the innocence, the simple times, the baby days. *"Time makes you bolder, children get older, and I'm getting older, too."* Damn you, Stevie Nicks. You sure knew what you were talking about.*

My children *are* getting older, and it's a little bittersweet. The good parts are easy to catalog: They can shower on their own and brush their own teeth, *halleluiah praise the high heavens.* We have deep and meaningful conversations about books and bugs and bullying and boys and life in general. They teach me new things, beyond song lyrics even, like how many sides a heptagon has (seven) and the fact that pterodactyls weren't in fact dinosaurs (they were flying reptiles, duh). They can pack and carry their own bags when we go on a trip, which is a major game changer if you ask me. They help around the house, give killer massages, and the things that come out of their mouths make me belly laugh on a daily basis. But still, I miss my babies.

I'm not going to do anything extreme like beg my husband to have his vasectomy reversed and try to get myself knocked up again, but I can see how some women get to that point. (And I'm nowhere *near* ready for grandchildren, so zip your lip or I will hurt you.) I'd never have believed it when I was in the thick of nursing and butt wiping and midnight wake-up

---

* I actually have no idea what she's talking about in that song. Ice climbing? Natural disasters? Did someone die? Break her heart? Still, for some reason that line always gets me. (But don't get me started on *revved up like a deuce.*)

calls and avocado mashing, but relatively speaking at least, babies are *easy*. They're soft and cuddly, and when they stick their tongues out at you, it's adorable. They can wear belly-baring T-shirts and ruffled underpants to the grocery store or the mall, and you don't have to worry about condescending stares or arrest warrants. You never have to watch their little spirits get crushed when a bitchy "friend" cuts them to the core with the cruelest insult she can fling, or worry about them being scared and lonely at a sleepover. They don't ask you about death and God and plane crashes and terrorism and other things you'd rather not talk about, if it's all the same. You don't stay up at night tossing and turning with the realization that your sister was right because *someday in the not-too-distant future* you're going to have to let them go.

Just last week our neighbor's daughter left for college.

"I wonder how she's doing," Joe said the other day, gesturing toward their house.

"I think she's a wreck," I told him. "I've seen her standing in the driveway a few times, looking completely lost."

"I was talking about the *daughter*," Joe said.

"Betta? Oh, she's fine! She's off at college, having the time of her life. It's the poor mom you should feel sorry for."

Joe looked at me like I was nuts, which, well, ahem. *But it's not that far away*, you guys, the day I'm standing in my driveway looking lost and worrying the neighbors. I don't want my nest to be empty. Not even a little bit. *How can this even be a concern*, I wonder. I just had these babies yesterday.

But of course I didn't. I've been a mom for more than a

decade, almost a quarter of my life. And while obviously I'm glad that my daughters are strong and independent and becoming more so every day—that's the goal of this crazy ride, right?—I'd be lying if I said it didn't rip a tiny piece of my heart out when I reach for one of their hands to cross a street and they refuse to take it, or I see them making the my-mom's-crazy gesture (index finger twirling around the temple) to their friends when they think I'm not looking. My babies would never have done that.

My babies also would never do a naked-shimmy dance across the bathroom floor, and when I asked them what they were doing, reply, "Oh, I'm just trying to make my hiney jiggle like yours." (My tween children, however, apparently have no problem doing this.) They wouldn't beg me daily for iPhones ("I didn't get an iPhone until I was thirty-seven," I like to remind them) or nuzzle up to me in bed first thing in the morning and then promptly push me away shrieking "Gross, Mom, it smells like poo is coming out of your mouth!" They wouldn't ask me why I have stripes on my forehead ("Because of you, kid. *Because of you.*") or why my boobs point down instead of out (See "the stripes on my forehead"). They certainly would never ask if they could borrow my favorite shirt—a baby! In a grown woman's shirt! Can you imagine?—and then rock that shirt so hard that I would be forced to relinquish it on the spot, because it's not like I could ever wear it again after seeing that. My babies wanted to be with me 24/7, a fact that I found stifling at the time but now secretly sort of miss.

Recently I decided to undertake the not-insignificant task of converting all of our home movie tapes to DVDs. If you are considering doing this, I recommend *not* embarking on the project while you are PMSing or otherwise hormonally imbalanced, as I have found that the sight of your diapered babes sitting on your young lap can bring you to sobbing, heaving tears. There we are running in the sprinklers and reading a book and baking cupcakes and reading another book. We're opening Christmas presents and blowing out candles and stacking blocks for the express purpose of knocking them down so we can stack them again. *We sure have a lot of energy invested in these kids,* I think as I watch clip after clip. *And the whole point is hopefully to do such a good job that they don't need us at all.*

I look at the way other people parent their kids, and I try not to judge. Fine, I totally judge. Because honestly, you guys, when you get your kid her very own iPad or a brand-new electric scooter or take her to see Katy Perry, I have to hear about it, okay? And I do not think you're doing your children any favors when you hand them everything they want the nanosecond they think about wanting it, even if it's in an Amazon .com box and not on a silver platter. Me? I'm sort of a bitch mom. My kids have to do daily chores (the whining!), and they don't get an allowance (the moaning!), because I want them to understand that they have responsibilities to this family simply by virtue of being a member of it. I'll pay them to unload the dishwasher and make their beds and put away their toys the day somebody starts compensating *me* to grocery shop, fold laundry, cook dinner, pull eleven miles of hair out of the shower drain every month, chisel petrified toothpaste out of multiple sink bowls, wipe the dogs' nose prints off the French doors a dozen times a week, and perform all of the other countless housekeeping tasks I do daily (mostly) without complaint. Not that I'm bitter.

"But Madison gets an allowance!" my woefully deprived daughters pout.

"Madison's mom must be nicer than I am," I reply.

"You can say *that* again," they mutter under their collective breath.

"Well, I *was* going to get you guys a pony," I lie, "but maybe you should ask Madison's mom to get it for you instead, since she's so flipping *nice*."

I remember being in college and hearing the infamous Mark Twain quote on parenting for the first time: "When I was a boy of fourteen," Twain wrote, "my father was so ignorant I could hardly stand to have the old man around. But when I got to be twenty-one, I was astonished at how much the old man had learned in seven years." This exact epiphany happened to me. Fast-forward another twenty years and put me on the other side of the equation with children of my own, however, and I had an equally surprising newsflash: *My parents had no idea what they were doing, either!* We're all just winging it, figuring it out as we go, and doing the best we can. Sometimes we'll screw up (see bit about Mandatory Pregnancy Permits for Unwed Mothers™, sorry Cori), and in all likelihood we'll be so desperate to do things differently than our parents did that we'll swing dangerously far in the opposite direction. My parents swore like sailors (I know, you're shocked) and didn't lay down much in the way of rules or boundaries; in my house "stupid" is a bad word,* and we have rules about how we'll implement our rules.

Am I screwing up my kids irreparably? Only time will tell. Good thing I'm probably only halfway dead, because I really can't wait to find out.

---

* I know, I'm such a hypocrite. Don't tell them, okay?

CHAPTER 20

When Did Construction Workers Become So Civilized?

As a builder's kid, I grew up around scores of dirty, sweaty, crude men whose other job, when they weren't swinging their hammers, was to objectify women—loudly and often. Most of the time when I was on a construction site, I was with my dad (their boss), so even the most boorish of his employees knew not to comment on my boobs or my ass or suggest we jump in his truck and do something unmentionable. But occasionally, like the time I stopped by one of his houses when I was riding my bike home from the beach—in a bikini, can you imagine?—these shirtless cauldrons of testosterone would unleash a string of X-rated catcalls in my direction before my dad showed up and their brains had a chance to register the words *BOSS'S DAUGHTER*. Dad would go ballistic, the rest of us would be mortified, and eventually, I was prohibited from flaunting my half-naked body within a five-mile radius of any of his jobs.

In case you missed the point of that story, *my* half-naked body elicited an excited reaction from young, strapping men!

Ah, those were the days.

Listen, Gloria Steinem disciples, I know your underarm hair is going to get all bunched when I say this, but I'd pay good money to get an unsolicited wolf whistle these days. A head turn as I'm sitting at a stoplight would be heavenly. Hell, when the cute Whole Foods cashier asks "How's your day going?" and not "How's your day going, *ma'am*?" I trot out to my car with a visible spring in my step.

It's ridiculous, I realize, to pine for supplementary opposite-gender attention for any number of reasons. For one thing, my husband tells me constantly that he thinks I'm hot. But as I've mentioned, seeing as my increasingly shapeless ass is the only one he gets to spoon for basically the rest of ever, complimenting me in this way serves two very important purposes: the first obviously is foreplay, and the second is probably a subconscious manifestation of "if I say it enough, I'll believe it, too!" I don't mean to belittle his words or imply that he *isn't* attracted to me. But my husband is a smart guy, and if a daily "hey, hottie" seems to increase his odds of getting laid even infinitesimally, he'll put it in the permanent rotation.

The other reason it's ridiculous to wish male strangers would publically declare their physical attraction to me is because, well, consider the source. With all due respect, the dudes crooning "ow, ow, ow, baby's on fire, gotta get me summa that" from the rooftops probably aren't that discriminating (and frankly, rarely look like the infamous Diet Coke Break commercial guy*). In fact, as often as not they have more back hair than my Labrador and are missing several key front teeth. Still, sometimes a slightly stale leftover cupcake is better than no dessert at all, if you know what I mean.

There's a saying that people in relationships use to justify what they consider harmless flirting: "Just because you're on a diet doesn't mean you can't look at the menu." Well, my happily married, utterly-content-but-maybe-just-a-tiny-bit-needy midlife version of that saying goes like this: "Just because you don't want the job doesn't mean you wouldn't enjoy repeatedly turning down the offer."

"But catcalling is derogatory, demeaning, and disrespectful!" you cry. I completely agree. Really, I do. And if we could stop it altogether, across the board, I'd be out there campaigning with you. But it does exist and it always will. And I don't know about you, but I'd rather not have to think of myself as someone no stranger would ever, if even for a fleeting drunken second in a mostly darkened room, want to (much less publically announce that he would like to) have sex with or even see naked.

(Unfortunately related aside: Just recently I was saying some-

---

* The one where all the office gals gather at exactly eleven thirty to watch the construction worker take off his shirt and enjoy his daily Diet Coke break. It's on Google, I just checked for you. Shit, how do you get drool out of a keyboard anyway?

thing about my "birthday suit" when it became apparent that my eight-year-old had never heard the term. When I explained what it was, she replied, "Oh! I thought you were talking about your birthday *dress*," referring to a sequin number I'd worn for my birthday party and which she had already decided was going to be hers when she grew up. After we laughed about the confusion, she hugged me sweetly and leaned in really close, cupping her hands around my ear. "No offense, Mom," she whispered, "but your birthday dress is *way* cuter than your birthday suit." Sadly, she's right.)

It doesn't seem all that terribly long ago that I was single and bar-trolling and being hit on with remarkable frequency. With my unlined face and perky boobs and without a guy on my arm or a ring on my finger, men would buy me drinks, pay me compliments, and often, drop really bad pickup lines on me. (My favorite: "Those jeans look great on you . . . but they'd look even better in a puddle on my floor.") When I shot these guys down, they'd move down to the next bar stool, and I'd sigh heavily at the inconvenience of being interrupted from the very important task of drinking with my girlfriends and hoping to get hit on. The last time a guy bought me a drink in a bar was on a girls' trip to Palm Springs, when my friends and I met a party of very fun, very wealthy, very old, very gay men who were clearly in the market for some middle-aged fruit flies.*

---

* The Internet seems to think that *other* term for females who love flaming men—the one that rhymes with "rag bag"—is now considered highly offensive and derogatory, which is too bad because it's really fun to say.

I have countless newly single pals who bemoan the miserable reality of having to jump back into the midlife dating pool—the one where you're swimming alongside Megan Fox lookalikes in itty-bitty bikinis who are hoping to catch the eye of the same fifty-year-old lifeguard as you are. Sure, my fabulous friends are infinitely smarter, significantly more accomplished, radically better traveled, substantially more solvent, profoundly more confident, doubtless better in bed,* and a thousand times sexier and more comfortable in their respective skin than their barely legal poolmates. Tragically, this particular contest doesn't have talent, evening wear, onstage question, *or* personal interview portions. It's a swimsuit competition all the way, and guess who's going to win pretty much every time? No really, guess.

[Calls husband, begs him to swear on bottomless cases of beer and a lifetime of blowjobs that he will never, ever leave her. Mercifully, he agrees.]

It's probably not as bad as I think it is. Surely there are at least a handful of not-disgusting guys out there, as the epic Leslie Mann character so awkwardly put it in the hilarious movie *This Is Forty*, who would gladly do sex with me, even though I'm pretty sure I've made it clear that I *do not want to do sex with any of them*. Or maybe there aren't. That is why sometimes I worry, when I lie in bed at night and mentally

---

* I can't say for sure, but I think we can assume they've picked up a few tricks along the way.

script my future only-slightly-fictionalized life movie,* that
this scene will have to be included:

EXT.—CUTE SUBURBAN SOUTHERN CALIFORNIA
NEIGHBORHOOD WITH MOSTLY QUAINT, OLDER HOMES
BUT ONE IN THE VERY EARLY STAGES OF NEW
CONSTRUCTION—DAY.

JENNA, a modestly attractive woman in her mid-
forties exits her front door with a dog on a
leash and walks up her driveway to the
sidewalk.† She stops, looks around as if
deciding which way to go, spots the house under
construction. She squares her shoulders, sucks
in her stomach, reaches down into her blouse to
shift her breasts up higher and closer together,
and starts marching toward the house, trying to
look cute and casual.

Despite the fact that there are no fewer than a
dozen men working on the house, not a single
one of them notices JENNA. She slows her gait,
still nothing. She clears her throat. One guy

---

* The really funny one starring Kristen Wiig as me and Will Arnett as Joe.
You do this, too, right?

† In the movie, the dog is a darling little *male* Boston terrier who is impossibly well behaved and doesn't leave piss burns all over my grass. In real
life, she's an ill-behaved, hyper black lab who sheds enough fur to build a
brand-new dog every three days and whose favorite food is my sparkliest
pair of Havaianas.

looks up then immediately back down. JENNA is walking so slowly she's barely even moving.

> **JENNA**
> A-a-a-*chooo*!

A few more sawdust-speckled heads peek up, briefly, before returning to their tasks.

JENNA makes it to the end of the street, turns around, and begins the painful, slow death march past the workers again. This time she tries swinging her hips and whistling. Nothing. Now back in front of her own home, JENNA unbuttons the top button on her blouse, then the next one. She does the up-and-in boob thing again, rolls up her shorts a few times, twists her car's side-view mirror down to see what this looks like, and quickly rolls them back down. Again, JENNA crawl-strolls past the house, willing her adorable dog to take a poop so she can linger. The little bastard refuses. Completely out of ideas, JENNA begins whistling an AC/DC tune, softly at first and then louder and louder. (She lived in New York City for a while and learned how to whistle really well, as it was the only reliable way to catch a cab during rush hour.) Finally, she manages to catch the attention of one of the construction workers, who is staring at her with his mouth agape. *Bingo!*

> ### HOT CONSTRUCTION WORKER 1
> Um, ma'am?

JENNA tries to flip her hair seductively, but
her watch gets stuck in it. She flails and pulls
at it for several seconds, looking as if a
spider has landed on her or perhaps she is
having some sort of seizure.

> ### HOT CONSTRUCTION WORKER 2
> *[whispering to HOT CONSTRUCTION
> WORKER 1]*
>
> Dude, what the fuck are you *doing*?

> ### HOT CONSTRUCTION WORKER 1
> *[whispering back]*
>
> Maybe she's hurt. Or sick.

> ### HOT CONSTRUCTION WORKER 2
> Or she just escaped from the loony bin.

> ### HOT CONSTRUCTION WORKER 1
> *[Ignoring him and cupping his hands
> around his mouth to call to Jenna]*
>
> Ma'am? Ma'am, are you okay? Are you lost?
> Do you need some help? Should we call
> someone for you?

JENNA looks around and behind her, trying to
figure out who these men could be talking to. She
spins around in circles several times, looking

for an old lady who appears to be lost or hurt;
the men start to look more concerned. Finally,
JENNA realizes what's happening. *She's the ma'am.*
Horror washes over her face as she runs like a
Kenyan sprinter, dragging her dog down the
sidewalk, up her driveway, and straight into her
front door, which she slams behind her.

> **HOT CONSTRUCTION WORKER 2**
> Dude, that was gnarly. I mean, I hope
> she's okay.

> **HOT CONSTRUCTION WORKER 1**
> Same shit happened to my mom when she got
> old. It's really sad.

CUT TO:

JENNA is lying in bed sobbing; her husband JOE
is trying to console her.

> **JOE**
> Oh, honey, of *course* you're still hot. Men
> have . . . evolved, is all. Guys just
> don't whistle at strange women on the
> street anymore. It's like a thing. I saw
> it . . . on the news.

> **JENNA**
> I sat in the front window for three hours
> today and watched those guys whistle at
> thirteen women. *Thirteen!* I counted.

> ### JOE
> Well, yeah . . . see . . . that's because they can tell that you're different. They respect you. That's it! They totally re-spect you in a way they'd never respect some young, hot—oh. Fuck.

JENNA rolls over and sobs facedown into her pillow. JOE looks at the camera, shaking his head, clearly thinking *WTF do I do now*?

CUT TO:

JOE is on a ladder leaning up against the house, working on the siding, and wearing a tool belt. He's shirtless and looking pretty damned good for a fifty-year-old, it's worth noting. JENNA comes walking out of the house, purse over her shoulder, and begins heading toward her car in the driveway.

> ### JOE
> *[whistles loudly]*
>
> Ow, ow, ow! That's a tight little ass, baby! I'd like to get me a piece of *that*. Hey, can I get some fries with that shake?

> ### JENNA
> *[shaking her head sadly]*
>
> Thanks, honey. But it's not the same.

CUT TO:

At the construction site, JOE is chatting with
HOT CONSTRUCTION WORKERS 1 and 2.

> **HOT CONSTRUCTION WORKER 1**
> So, let me get this straight: When your
> wife walks or even drives by, you want us
> to shout vulgar obscenities at her?

> **JOE**
> Yes, please!

> **HOT CONSTRUCTION WORKER 2**
> Every time?

> **JOE**
> If it's not too much trouble, that would
> be great.

> **HOT CONSTRUCTION WORKER 1**
> Do you want, like, slightly vulgar or
> really nasty?

> **JOE**
> Let's go with really nasty.

> **HOT CONSTRUCTION WORKER 1**
> And you promise this isn't some sort of
> setup?

> **JOE**
> I swear it on my life.

                      HOT CONSTRUCTION WORKER 2
And you're not going to call the cops or
come over here and try to kick our asses?
I mean, not that you *could* or anything,
but you're not even going to try?

                      JOE
      *[one hand to heart, the other held up
      Boy Scout style]*

I will not summon any law enforcement of-
ficers or lay a finger on any one of you,
so help me God.

                      HOT CONSTRUCTION WORKER 1
You said fifty bucks apiece, right?

                      JOE
I did. But you guys seem legit. Let's make
it seventy-five.

                      HOT CONSTRUCTION WORKER 1
Sweet, man!

                      HOT CONSTRUCTION WORKER 2
You got a deal.

JOE reaches for his wallet, doles out the cash.
The dudes look pretty stoked.

CUT TO:

In a déjà vu repeat of the opening scene, JENNA exits her front door with her darling little dog on a leash and walks up her driveway to the sidewalk. This time she's wearing high heels, a super-short skirt and a skintight tank top over a leopard push-up bra. She looks fairly ridiculous as she stops and looks purposefully toward the house under construction. JENNA squares her shoulders, sucks in her stomach, rearranges her boobs, and starts marching toward the house, trying to look somewhat young and extremely slutty.

> **HOT CONSTRUCTION WORKER 1**
> *[whispering to HOT CONSTRUCTION WORKER 2]*

Hey, here she comes!

> **HOT CONSTRUCTION WORKER 2**
> *[shouting]*

Hey there, pretty lady!

> **HOT CONSTRUCTION WORKER 1**
> *[whispering to HOT CONSTRUCTION WORKER 2]*

Pretty lady? Really? Dude, you suck at this. The husband said to be *nasty*!

                    HOT CONSTRUCTION WORKER 2
            [whispering to HOT CONSTRUCTION
            WORKER 1]

    I know, but she's *old*. I don't want her to
    have a heart attack or anything.

                [trying again, this time yelling at
                JENNA]

    Nice legs, gorgeous. You want to come up here
    and wrap 'em around me?

    And when you're done, maybe I can pet your dog!

                [winks suggestively]

                    HOT CONSTRUCTION WORKER 1
            [whispering to HOT CONSTRUCTION
            WORKER 2 again]

        Seriously, man, just stop. Stop now.

    JENNA hears them, looks around again, this time
    to make sure they're talking to her. They are!
    She tries to conceal her glee and in fact look
    disgusted. She does a lousy job at both. They
    continue to catcall, getting progressively more
    vulgar,* as JENNA oh-so-slowly makes her way
    past the house. Finally, she is almost out of
    sight.

    _____

    * Use your imagination, okay? My mother is probably going to read this.

    . . . .

> **HOT CONSTRUCTION WORKER 2**
> *[shouting]*
>
> Hummina, hummina! Lookin' fine from be-
> hind, too!

A huge smile breaks out across JENNA'S face. *Oh
yeah, she's still got it.*

FADE TO BLACK . . .

That would be sad, right?

Although it's impossible to fathom that it went down more than half of my lifetime ago, one of my favorite attempted-pickup stories happened to me in my twenties. I was at a bar (naturally) with a bunch of girlfriends and this one guy would not leave me alone. He'd asked me to dance, offered me a seat, and begged to buy me a drink a dozen or more times. I had turned him down in each case, because I could tell he'd barnacle himself to my leg if I so much as let him give me his advanced spot in the mile-long bathroom line. At one point in the evening, I was at the bar ordering more drinks (of course), when I felt a tap on my shoulder and turned around. It was him, wanting to know if I was *sure* I wouldn't let him get this round.

"I'm good, thanks," I told him, turning back around and placing my order.

Tap, tap, tap.

"Just one?" he pleaded. "What's the big deal?"

Having answered this question thirteen times already, I decided to ignore him. Just as the bartender set down my order, I felt a hand slide down my back, land on my ass, and give it a hearty squeeze. Without even stopping to think, I grabbed a full drink in each fist, spun around, and threw them both in the guy's face.

"Um," he whimpered, and with alcohol dripping from his hair and eyelashes and lips, he motioned behind him with one hand. "That was your friend."

Sure enough, my pal Allison was standing directly behind him. Allison raised her hand as if someone had asked who was responsible for this situation. She looked simultaneously horrified, guilty, and as if she was doing everything in her power not to break out into a fit of hysterical laughter. I apologized profusely to the sticky stranger and wound up buying his drink. As I'd feared, that soaking wet SOB totally took advantage of the situation and clung to me like an injured tree frog all night. Lesson learned.*

A decade later in my thirties, when I was still occasionally getting asked to show my ID to buy booze, I'd always think, "I wonder if this is the last time I'll ever get carded." Eventually, it was. Now I think, "I wonder if that's the last time I'll ever get to throw a drink in someone's face."

So far, it is. But you never know.

---

* The lesson being I was right and that you should never give a guy (that you don't ever want to have sex with) an inch.

·····················

CHAPTER 21

The Big Chill Was Bullshit

Despite my affinity for profanity (or perhaps because of it?) I never had any trouble making friends when I was single. After all, it wasn't impossibly hard to find somebody I liked well enough to go to a yoga class with or sit next to in a movie or maybe even go away with for a weekend. If I met a woman who was funny, prompt, smart, not too political or religious, and could fork over her half of the dinner tab, she'd probably at least make it onto the long list.

Then I met the man who would become my husband. Of course I kept all of my old friends and Joe kept his, and everyone was welcomed warmly into the growing fold. We got engaged, bought a house, and moved in together, then we embarked on that obnoxious new-couple nesting phase where we wanted to be alone together morning and night, and had little need for outside interference or entertainment. We had everything we needed, and "make fun new friends" slid to the very bottom of our collective to-do lists.

While we were extremely busy inspecting each other's every pore and making googly eyes at one another, our friends were out trolling the streets for life partners of their own. *Because that's what you do.* Joe and I were excited about this because, frankly, after a while tables for two get old, and when you both know every answer to every question in Cranium, the game sort of loses its appeal. We wanted other cool, like-minded couples to do exciting and adventurous new things with, and we clung to the hope that one of our many friends would come through for us and bring some fun, fresh blood to the mix. We pictured traveling dinner parties and potluck barbecues and that dancing-around-the-kitchen-island scene from *The Big Chill* (minus the dead guy), because that was totally grown-up and sophisticated and *so were we*. It was only a matter of weeks before our fantasies promptly began the journey to hell in the proverbial handbasket.*

"Bob's engaged," Joe announced in a neutral voice one night.

---

* If, like me, you've wondered why a small, portable, handheld container was chosen as the underworld's preferred delivery system, apparently back in the guillotine days, handbaskets were used to catch the severed heads of the mortally wounded. And obviously, since the slain subjects had committed a crime punishable by death, they were going straight to hell. Don't you feel better knowing that? I sure do.

"Not to Shelby, I hope," I replied. Bob had been dating Shelby for as long as I'd known him, and nobody liked her. Not his parents or his siblings or any of his friends or even our dog Sam, who loved everybody. Clearly, Bob had had the good sense to dump her ass and find a more likeable replacement, whom I couldn't wait to meet.

"Yup, to Shelby," Joe said.

"But *why*?" I wanted to know. Shelby was uptight and pinch faced and hanging out with her was about as enjoyable as a cold bikini wax. The first time we had her over to our house—which was 1,100 square feet of pure charm, I might add—she looked around haughtily and said, "I *wish* I could live in a tiny house. It must be so nice not to have to walk very far to get anything."

I am not making this up. She said that. To my face. *In my home.* Clearly Bob and Shelby were never going to be invited over for game night or even a Super Bowl party. It was too bad, too, because Bob was funny and smart, *and* he had a boat.

The thing was, I discovered, when you're half of a couple, finding another twosome to hang out with is approximately forty-seven billion times harder than finding a partner was. You pretty much have to weed through the planet's entire population to unearth two sets of previously paired people who enjoy spending time with each other equally or at least close to it. I don't exactly know how to calculate the chances of that happening, but for comparative purposes, consider that the odds of rolling a four of a kind with four dice are 6 in 1,296, or 0.005 percent. In other words, you'd be a fool to bet the house on it.

Despite those abysmal odds, Joe and I eventually managed to find a handful of couples we both enjoyed socializing with in our newlywed days. We had dinner parties just like we'd fantasized about and took lake and ski trips and shared holiday meals with this posse of like-minded homies, and once when a group of us were cleaning up the kitchen, "Ain't Too Proud to Beg" came on, and we all nearly lost it. All was well and right with the world, and even though all of our biological relatives were far away, Joe and I had created for ourselves a hybrid family that was entirely of our choosing. We stopped short of drawing blood from our wrists and comingling the fluids (you did this with your best girlfriends in elementary school so that you could be "blood sisters" too, right?), but we were nevertheless fully and forever committed.

And then everybody started having babies, and it was like somebody strapped a turbo jetpack onto the back of the hand-basket and it blasted our friendships straight to the bottomless pit of the netherworld.

I might be being slightly melodramatic there, but honestly, nothing can break up an ongoing platonic orgy faster than suddenly finding yourselves on opposite sides of the parenting chasm. Teetering on one edge you've got your couple who's so utterly engrossed in this new baby world that they don't realize that a mere year ago they would have been repulsed by any conversation that had the words *mucus plug* or *placenta* in it, too. They refuse to go anywhere loud or crowded, their minivan smells like moldy milk, and they have to be home by seven p.m. to protect their tot's precious sleep schedule. On the other side, you've got your freewheeling, unencumbered, still-spontaneous pair who try their best to dote on the adorably dressed blob in the room but frankly can't wait to return her to her parents and belly back up to the bar.

Eventually though, the partiers probably decide to procreate, too, and once their own bundle arrives, they get it. They laugh with the duo that trod the parenting path before them, and apologize for being so insensitive that time they didn't give their pals enough lead time to find a babysitter for their New Year's Eve party. The forerunners forgive them, of course, and show their amnesty by inundating the initiates with a nonstop parade of gently used bouncy seats and baby monitors and travel cribs. The four adults, high on bonding hormones and lack of sleep, take a zillion pictures of their offspring together, fantasizing about a new generation of lifelong friendships and—in the happiest and most perfect of all worlds—marriage.

"We could be in-laws!" they cry, propping little Piper up against Preston for another photo shoot. "Ooh," the photographer squeals, showing the group the money shot where Preston is holding Piper's tiny hand and looking sweetly into her eyes. "This one will be perfect to blow up at the wedding!"

The happy-family bliss bubble continues to grow exponentially, up until right around the time Preston starts walking and talking. Hopefully everyone is wearing safety goggles and raincoats when he does, because this is when that deceptively delightful bubble pops. And it turns out, the bubble is filled with several shit-tons of bitter envy and resentment.

"That Preston is a goddamned *animal*," Piper's dad

grumbles through a fake smile as he waves good-bye to Preston's family out the front window. "Did you see him jumping on my new leather chair in his filthy shoes?"

"I did," Piper's mom replies. "And you missed it when he was hitting Piper on the head with his stuffed dinosaur. He could have given her a concussion! And the worst part was those parents of his didn't even try to stop him! They have no rules whatsoever. How can you have no rules? Mark my words: Preston is going to grow up to be a nightmare, a total nightmare. Maybe it's best if we don't have them over anymore."

Meanwhile, over in Preston's car, his mother sits smugly in the front seat, shaking her head and tsk-tsking.

"She's bottle feeding Piper, can you *believe* it?" she sighs. "It wasn't easy, you know, but I nursed Preston for *twenty-eight weeks.* Breast milk is so much better for babies; it really is a shame she didn't even try."

"Did they even thank us for the soothing tropical rain forest sounds CD we brought?" Preston's dad wants to know. "I made that myself."

"Not that I heard," Preston's mom says. "And I hate to say it, but I think there may be something wrong with Piper, too. Did you see how she just sits there like a lump, doing nothing? And she's four months old! Preston was rolling over *and* clapping his hands at that age, remember? It's probably because they never turn their TVs off. Did you notice that, too? They have a TV in every room, and they're all blaring constantly. All of that stimulation isn't good for a child. I don't know if we should hang around with them anymore."

That lucky sonofabitch does *have a TV in every room, doesn't he?* Preston's dad thinks, but he says nothing. Obviously he is going to need to bring this up at a much more opportune time.

From here, the group lovefest is on a downhill slippery slope paved with disparate views on spanking, vaccinating, and buying organic, on Ferber's versus Sears's approach to sleep, cloth versus disposable diapers, public versus private education, hand sanitizer versus germs as immunity boosters, listening to your body versus cleaning your plate, and what exactly is the right age to get your kid a cell phone. And even though every child is different and there is no one perfect way to parent,* tensions rise and tempers flare every time there's a parental impasse. All four parties sit and marvel at the fact that these people they thought they had so much in common with could turn out to be colossal flops in such an important department.

Once your spawn start talking and having opinions and playmates and a far busier social calendar than you've got, it gets even harder. Now you don't just need to find a couple that you and your partner like equally and whose parenting approach you both approve of; now you're tasked with finding all of that *plus* these people must have the perfect children who must be roughly the same age(s) and exactly the same gender(s) as yours. Sure, you could go ahead and plan an evening of fun for your four- and six-year-old girls and their nine-, eleven-, and seventeen-year-old boys. Just be prepared to be interrupted

---

* Although mine comes pretty close, so maybe I should write a book about it?

every thirty seconds to deflect another complaint of "we have nothing to doooo" and "when can we go hoooome?"

Eventually you may just resign yourself to the fact that it's easiest if your pals are your children's friend's parents. It's almost a default setting, a path of least resistance. These friendships build slowly, mostly by sitting next to the same faces at 2,394 spring sings, potluck picnics, back-to-school barbecues, soccer games, dance recitals, PTA meetings and promotions. "Hey, I forgot my camera," you might lie to the seemingly normal woman whose name you can never remember and aren't sure which kids she goes with (but pray it isn't the twins with the deadly nut allergies). "If I give you my email address, would you mind sending me copies of yours?"

She actually follows through, and you wind up exchanging some witty emails. After she drops the f-bomb in one and alludes to being hungover in another, you decide to get serious about the pursuit. Now that you are officially courting her, you suggest to your husband that you should have them over for dinner.

"But we don't even know them!" he shouts in a panic.

"I realize that, dear," you reply calmly. "That's why I suggested we have them over."

"Well, what if they're freaks?" he asks, because apparently he's had one too many freaky get-togethers and is extremely gun shy about a repeat performance.

"It's two hours, not a bike trip across Europe," you remind him. "They might be lovely. They *seem* lovely."

"That's what you said about the Andersons and look how *that* turned out," he scoffs.

"How was I supposed to know they were swingers?" you demand. "It's not like they were wearing swinger uniforms or anything."

"I told you the day we met them that he wanted you," he says.

"You say that about everyone!" you insist.

"And I was *right*!" he says triumphantly.

"Can I invite the McNormals over for dinner or not?" you sigh.

"Let's meet them somewhere," he counters. "I don't want them in my house if they turn out to be freaks."

"Thank you for making this both simple and fun," you say.

Unless the McNormals are in fact swingers or Mr. M tries to get you to sign up under him in "this awesome new multi-level marketing scheme—which, trust him, isn't like any of the other ones you've tried before," you'll socialize on occasion because you have the same school breaks and can maybe even get an occasional afternoon of free babysitting or a carpool out of the deal. You may not love them, but if you like them even close to moderately, they'll probably get thrown into the social rotation. It's just so easy and convenient that you can't really fight it.

Unless they have Food Issues, that is.

I am pretty sure Food Issues destroy more platonic relationships than lying, stealing, backstabbing, borrowing and ruining favorite sweaters, and gossiping combined. My friend Paula recently ended a thirty-year friendship over a pair of granola bars, I shit you not. To celebrate a joint milestone birthday, she'd taken her two kids to visit an old college friend. To protect this friend's identity, I'll just refer to her as That Smug Bitch. That Smug Bitch has two kids also, and apparently these children have never eaten a morsel of processed food in their entire lives. Think about that: These *teenagers* have never had a crumb of an Oreo cookie, a sip of Slurpee, or even a single Spaghetti-O pass their lips. They down wheatgrass smoothies happily and without complaint, nibble on raw kale and almonds from their backyard garden when they get the munchies, and would have no idea what it means to have a disembodied voice tell you to "pull up to the next window."

"You should have seen That Smug Bitch when I gave the kids a couple of granola bars from my purse," Paula told me, over wine of course. "They were starving to death, what was I supposed to do? That Smug Bitch acted like I was giving them a crack pipe, for crying out loud. And they were *organic* granola bars, too."

Despite decades of history and similar views on everything from religion and politics to paper versus plastic, it took Paula all of two days to realize that she and That Smug Bitch no longer had enough in common to sustain even a superficial friendship.

"Yeah, I feed my kids macaroni and cheese," Paula huffed. "And crackers I didn't bake with stone-ground wheat from my backyard, too. That Smug Bitch doesn't even work! She has no *idea* what the real world is like. And I don't care what she says, her kids do not *love* lima beans. Nobody loves lima beans. She's a fucking liar."

"One time when I was paying to get out of a parking garage," I told Paula, "my oldest daughter leaned forward from the backseat and shouted 'Can I please have French fries and a chocolate shake?' You know, because she thought we were at In-N-Out."

"That's why we will always be friends," Paula told me.

I topped off her glass and gave her a hug, because that's what friends do.

CHAPTER 22

Are We Happy Yet?

Remember when I mentioned that I have the uncanny ability to retain utterly useless information? Well, because of that, esteemed psychologist Abraham Maslow's colorful, pyramid-shape hierarchy of needs is permanently imprinted on my brain. In case you're not familiar with it—or it's one of the bits from your past that you've managed to successfully purge—the hierarchy is a visual list of man's greatest motivators, based on the belief that only when certain needs are met are we able to move up to the next level of our physical, mental, and spiritual evolution.

At the bottom of the pyramid are your most basic physiological requirements: breathing, food, water, sex, sleep, excretion. Clearly, if your bowels are backed up to your neck or your canteen springs a leak halfway through your trans-Saharan trek, or you're in the middle of being suffocated, you're not going to be compelled to ask your boss for a raise or write your memoirs at that particular moment. Only as each level of needs is met do you get to claw your way closer to the top, where all of the good stuff is.

After the life-or-death needs come issues regarding safety (shelter, order, employment, money). Next, if you're definitely breathing and have a roof over your head, you can date and socialize. Now that you've got a pulse, a home, a job, and a partner, you are freed up to focus on matters related to your self-esteem (confidence, achievement, respect). Finally, at the tippy-top of the pyramid—where it's presumed you have secured every last item in the fat triangle beneath you—you are invited to self-actualize. This apex of the motivational chain includes inner growth, spiritual enlightenment, the pursuit of knowledge, and the enjoyment of creative expression. According to Maslow, once the pressing needs for cheeseburgers, door locks, decent human beings in your life with which you interact regularly, and a complete obliteration of any self-loathing have been met, you are free to focus on the pursuit of that elusive SOB known as happiness.

The hierarchy theory may help explain why a recent Gallup poll of more than 340,000 people found that after a certain age—namely the mid-century mark—happiness doesn't just go up, it *keeps* going up. Even as our hair is falling out and our boobs are settling in around our waists and we can't remember what day of the week it is anymore, we're quietly becoming a bunch of giddy old loons who are only going to get ever giddier. Ostensibly this is because by this point, we've managed to work our way up through much of that pesky pyramid, ticking off the more mundane matters of existence. Our bases neatly covered, we get to enjoy the luxury of happiness—or at least our guaranteed right to the pursuit of it.

Before the midlife point—when we're plumbing the depths of that pyramid—if you were to map median happiness levels on a graph, it would look a lot like an *inverted* pyramid. Globally speaking, people seem to enter adulthood feeling modestly good about being above ground and upright. Then the shit hits the proverbial fan. Life gets hard and complicated (or at least harder and more complicated). Satisfaction starts to nosedive. We have to get jobs and pay our rent or mortgages and fork over our hard-earned earnings for annoying things like plungers and bite guards and car insurance and possibly find a suitable life partner, which we all know is no easy task. Then we pop out a few babies (ouch! and expensive!) and get laid off from the job we hated anyway and maybe get a divorce or find a lump or our parents die. *This sucks,* we mutter, as body parts we never really thought about before start hurting and we wonder how on earth we're going to be able to survive on the sixteen dollars we've managed to save so far. "What's the *point*?" we wonder, often and loudly. Around this time we may experiment with (different) antidepressants or start drinking (more) or smoking (more) dope or get addicted to painkillers or Words with Friends or *Real Housewives of New Jersey*—anything to numb, diffuse, distract.

After we toil in this existential space for a few decades—frankly too busy to give our ranking on any happiness scale all that much thought—the tide starts to shift. We're probably not living on Ramen noodles and beer anymore, and we have at the very least moved from busboy to server. We're out of the terrifying diapers-and-choke-hazard phase of parenting and hopefully not living with our parents or off of them. We know who we are and what we like and what's important. We've learned to appreciate the fragile gift that is life and to move past our mistakes. Maybe we've lost a parent or two, or perhaps we're taking care of them, but either way we've faced the fact of our own mortality. (Oh, we don't like it, and we try not to think about it, but it's there, and we're more or less resigned to it.) By the time there are fifty candles on our birthday cakes, the survey above suggests, no matter what steaming, stinking, miserable sort of monkey poo life slings at us, the general consensus seems to be: "Yeah? Well, it beats the alternative (chuckle, chuckle)." As the inimitable Anna Quindlen put it, if we think of life as a job, most of us feel that after five decades of laboring, we've finally gotten pretty good at it. We are—dare we even say it?—happy.

Happiness is no longer just a nebulous goal; it's a science. As such, the get-there guide is constantly evolving. For instance, where scientists once told us we were all born with a happiness "set point" that was mostly a fixed entity, newer research suggests that while we're at least partially hardwired to be closer to one end or the other of the crabby-to-cheerful scale, we have control over as much as 40 percent of our happiness.

There are incalculable books, blogs, classes, and coaches eager to guide us along the paved-by-research path to contentment. From an admittedly arbitrary review of the research, I have handpicked some doable moves that actual studies suggest might make us all happier right this minute, or at least in the very near future if we're reading this while stuck in gridlocked traffic or in the middle of root canal surgery:

Laugh at that shit. Why do people flock to funny movies or pay money to see Jerry Seinfeld on stage or (hopefully) buy my books? Because laughing feels good. It reduces stress, increases oxygen flow, and even boosts metabolism. And life is pretty funny, when you think about it, even when things go horribly, miserably wrong. In fact, sometimes life is funniest *because* things go horribly, miserably wrong. But you only get all of those benefits if you can let out a hearty guffaw when they do.

Here's an example: We recently took a family vacation to the Florida Keys, which is pretty far from where we live and not exactly easy to get to. In order to save a few bucks on our plane tickets, we flew in and out of LAX, which is three hours away and a miserable clusterfuck on the best of all days. A visit to this particular airport ranks on my personal pleasure scale somewhere below filing my taxes and having a sharp metal stick repeatedly jabbed into my eye socket. There was a long drive on the other coast as well, making the door-to-door travel time twenty hours, horrifying even if we weren't going to have our kids in tow—which we were. I was thinking about all of this the night before we left as we were packing.

"So what do you think is going to be the Thing?" I asked my husband.

"The Thing?" Joe asked, giving me his famous I-hate-it-when-you're-cryptic-especially-when-I'm-stressed-out single-eyebrow raise.

"You know, *the Thing* that's going to go disastrously wrong but will turn out to be the Thing that we laugh about and associate with this trip for the rest of ever," I said simply. Because every trip we have ever taken has had a Thing. I'm not talking about missed flights or lost luggage or lodging that turned out to be slightly less fabulous than it looked online, although we're no strangers to any of those things. No, I'm talking about the terrible-at-the-time, how-will-we-ever-fix-this, can-you-even-believe-this-is-even-happening shit that we somehow manage to survive—and then enjoy reliving in glorious, horrific detail for the rest of our lives.

There was me waking up in the dirtiest city in Ireland with what I thought was a brain tumor (but turned out to be vertigo, which is nothing that a shot in the bum and two days of sleep can't fix right up). Getting separated from Joe on a hike in England and then being completely lost in the forest for several terrifying hours. The two of us being attacked by sea lice in the Bahamas and coming home with nasty, itchy, full-body rashes.* Every single person on my uncle's boat getting violently seasick, one after another, during a fishing trip in

---

* Yes, that's a thing. And it's as disgusting as it sounds.

Florida. The huge fight in Hawaii where I demanded Joe let me out of the car, *and he did*, right on the side of a very busy road, before peeling away and spraying me with gravelly dust. While each of these events was undeniably miserable in the moment, it nevertheless gets trotted out to great amusement any time the trip in question is mentioned.

"There's not going to be a Thing," Joe said with some irritation—plus what I considered a naïve amount of optimism.

Of course there was a Thing. There were several, in fact, but there are two in particular that already have become part of this particular trip's lore and aren't likely to be forgotten. The first was when we lost the rental car keys (we may have gotten a ride to a somewhat distant resort with some friends, where we may have pretended to be staying so we could hang out at their much nicer pool, and while we were there and enjoying their delicious frozen cocktails, we may have dropped the keys somewhere on the property without realizing it and then gotten a ride back to our own resort with our friends) and spent an entire day—and a hundred dollars in cab fare—looking for them. The second was when my husband, who is rather famous for not fucking up, locked *the same damned set of keys* in the rental car at midnight the night before we had to leave at five a.m. to catch our flight home. (Thank God for AAA is all I can say.) Although neither of these events was *at all* amusing in the moment, we've gotten great mileage—and plenty of laughter—out of our "keys in the Keys" stories. If you keep a little perspective, and hopefully are able to use life's minor tragedies as fodder for your next book or blog post, you might even go looking for disaster!

Be grateful. Happiness researchers point out over and over that the most cheerful souls are the ones who focus on and appreciate the things they *do* have, not lament the things they don't.* This is not always easy, of course, but it's considered one of the tippy-top tickets to bliss, so we all should really make more of an effort here. Let's give it a shot: Your job sucks? *At least you have one.* Oh, what? You don't have a job, either? *At least you've got your health.* You say you're sick as a dog? *At least you're not dead.* You might have to dig really deep to find that comparative thing to be thankful for, but it's always there. Even if you're dead (at least you don't have to go to that sucky job or feel like crap all the time anymore!). If all else fails, you can always resort to: *At least I was never married to Charlie Sheen.*†

Surround yourself with happy people. This doesn't merely mean you should purge your contact list of any assholes—although that's certainly a fine first step; you also have to *spend quality time* with people you love and who make you feel good. *[Puts "girls' night out—woohoo!" onto calendar; feels immediately happier.]*

Get the hell off of Facebook. I'm actually not kidding. Or, alternatively, if you're a glutton for punishment, put this book down and go peruse the timelines of your friends and

---

* Try it with me: "Yay! I have cellulite and a ton of debt!"

† If you're reading this, Brooke Mueller, Denise Richards, or Donna Peele, I'm sorry. Please change that to Jesse James.

take note of how thin and tan and successful and happy they are, how smiley and well-behaved their children appear, how doting their spouses are, and how many fabulous vacations to exotic far-flung locales they take. *Goddamnit, they're in Cabo right now, Instagramming sunset strolls and seaside massages and lobster dinners and miles of crystal clear water just beyond their perfectly painted toes.* "This place is truly magical," every other status update reads, *as if that's not perfectly fucking apparent from the 284 shots you just uploaded, thanks!* Even their dogs are cute and well groomed, and aren't drooling all over the kitchen floor like your mangy mutts are right this very minute.

Alas, Facebook is to real life what a staged model home is to an actual house that has living people cooking in its kitchen and sleeping in its beds and shitting in its toilets (and sometimes shitting in its beds). It's spit shined and digitally enhanced and, literally as well as metaphorically, *nobody lives there.* Your "friends" aren't posting photos of the night their teenager got busted for vandalism or the day their sewer line sprung a leak and flooded the entire front yard. Their vacation photos rarely show their kids fighting and whining in the three-hour airport security line even though you know it happened, and you almost never get to see the 278 outtakes it took to get that glowing, sun-kissed, happy-family picture that looks like the one that comes in the frame.

Actually, some people—like me, for instance—think Facebook is the *perfect* place to showcase life's crappiest moments, so we can all get a great laugh out of them together. So if you must indulge, I urge you to befriend cynics like me and not those fake-chipper bitches who Photoshop out every wrinkle before they post their pictures. They're not doing you any favors.

(It's worth noting that while I thought Facebook misery was just my personal theory, several weeks after I wrote that section I saw a headline on BBC News declaring "Facebook Use Undermines Well-being." The cause, according to researchers? Something known as FOMO, or Fear of Missing Out, a side effect of seeing your friends and family frolicking on exotic beaches while you're sitting at your computer in Hello Kitty pajamas. See? It's a *thing*, people. Just log off.)

Read about happiness studies. This one, for instance, cheered me up the instant I scanned it: Researchers at the University of Michigan discovered that blowing cold air up participants' noses put them in better moods than when they blew *hot* air up their noses. (Are you picturing this experiment? Honestly!) The takeaway here isn't necessarily that you should go snort some dry ice or even open your freezer and breathe deeply when you're in a pissy mood; I believe the real lesson is that we all need to appreciate the fact that we're *not participating in any sort of air-snorting studies* either currently or in the near future.

Do a good deed. Remember the movie *Pay It Forward*? Of course you do—it's not nearly as old as *Groundhog Day*. It's all about how random acts of kindness can change the world. If you're skeptical, consider what it can do to your mood when some jackass snakes around you and slides into the parking spot you've been waiting for, patiently, with your turn signal blinking and everything. Then think about how likely you are (very) to take your venomous rage home with you after that happens and unleash it on your nearest and dearest. Obviously our actions have a powerful impact on the people around us, even total strangers. You see those "hey, I paid for your dinner" notes on Pinterest, and you like and re-pin them with abandon, because even witnessing altruism and unsolicited generosity feels good. It turns out, practicing it feels even better.

This actually happened to me: One day I was in the local grocery store with my newborn baby, and I found myself in the checkout line behind a lady who was struggling to wrangle her three young children and unload her cart at the same time. At the time, I was pretty pleased with myself for making it out with a single unwieldy person in my care, and I watched her in awe. When the cashier had everything bagged up and gave the lady her total, she began fishing in her bag for her wallet.

She fished and she fished.

Her kids were starting to get antsy, and the lady was beginning to get embarrassed. After an eternity, she finally had to admit that she didn't have her wallet and would have to come back another time.

"But . . . but . . . your *stuff*!" I said to her.

She shrugged, looking utterly hopeless.

"But you got dressed, and you made it out of your house and got three kids in and out of their car seats, and you found everything you needed, and now you'll have to do it all over again!" I cried, visibly more upset than she was about the whole situation. (I blame postpartum hormones.)

The wallet-less lady began herding her kids toward the exit.

"I'll pay for it and you can pay me back," I called after her.

She turned around, surprised, hopeful, and slightly mortified all at the same time.

"Oh, I couldn't do that," she said with a little hesitation.

"Sure you could!" I insisted. "And you really should."

"How do you know I'm good for it?" she asked, inching back toward the register.

"I don't," I told her. "But it's sixty bucks. It won't kill me if you're not. But I sort of think you are."

Her grateful smile was worth three figures at least.

"I'm good for it," she said. "I promise."

I paid for her things, and I gave her my mailing address. I had no intention of telling my husband that I had done this, because I knew he'd call me a complete moron or at least think it.

Two days later, I got a check from her in the mail. With a gift card to a local smoothie shop, which apparently she owned. "You have no idea how much I appreciated that," she wrote on a sticky note, which I promptly and smugly showed to my husband, who didn't call me a moron but probably still thought it. I hope you don't think I'm blowing smoke up my own ass by telling you this story; I'm sharing it because the experience was a major high, not to mention a win-win, and I am grateful for having had that opportunity.

Eat some chocolate. Blah, blah, blah, something about antioxidants or serotonin or some other physiological phenom-

enon. Who cares? Chocolate is one of life's great pleasures.*
It's sensuous and decadent and impossibly satisfying, at least
if you get the good kind and especially if you mix it with
something salty. I'm not saying that inhaling a pound of
Godiva is going to bring you bliss; in fact, it might even bring
you to your knees in front of the nearest throne, and even if it
doesn't, it may paralyze you with guilt and self-loathing. But
I think we can all agree that it's impossible to feel happy and
deprived at the same time. Seriously. Eat some fucking chocolate.

Celebrate your resiliency. As the popular and impossibly
eloquent saying goes, shit happens. The fantastic news is that
when seriously sucky events transpire, human beings possess
a remarkable ability to bounce back, and with alarming speed.
I'm not talking about relatively minor miseries like breaking
an arm or losing out on a job promotion; according to resiliency research, had my home actually burned to the ground
during one of our many "evacucations," I would have made
peace with that fact and completely moved on with my life in
a matter of weeks. Sounds like a lot of horseshit, right? Consider a now-famous study that found that after devastating
accidents that confine people to wheelchairs for life, paraplegics
return to their pre-catastrophe levels of happiness within a
year.

---

* Chocolate can be a metaphor for lots of things, you know. This is about
indulging in something not overtly harmful every once in a while.

Think about that for a second. *People who lose the ability to walk get over it.* I don't know about you, but I spend a great deal of time worrying about things. This is insanely unproductive to begin with, because I tend to fret mostly about things that are beyond my control. But I really like the idea that should one of my worst-case scenarios actually happen, it more than likely won't throw me into an irreversible, lifelong depression.

Get yourself a black angel. Recently I was interviewing a renowned "happiness expert" for one of those "be happier" stories I write for women's magazines. The expert and I were discussing the very common midlife pursuit of the pinnacle of Maslow's pyramid when she threw me for a pretty major loop.

"The basic understanding of happiness is that it's outside of us," Dr. Aymee told me. "We promote 'go get happiness through these things or experiences,'* but that's actually very unhealthy. If you tell yourself you'll be happy when you leave work and go home, what happens when you get there and your husband is in a shitty mood and the kids are screaming and the toilet is overflowing? Your day is totally fucked.† The truth is that happiness is a choice that anyone can make, any time they want to, regardless of the circumstances."

"Oh really?" I said, probably a little more snidely than I'd

---

* I am pretty sure she means *shoes.*

† Yup, she said *totally fucked.* That's why I loved her immediately.

intended. (Actually I say that thing about happiness being a choice to my kids all the time. But I wasn't sure if I necessarily believed my own BS or if it was just a handy tool for deflecting and confusing my whiny children.) "This morning I woke up, poured my coffee, and then added rotten, curdled half-and-half to it," I added. "I had to throw the whole thing away. Trust me, I was not happy."

"Because you *chose* not to be happy," Dr. Aymee insisted. "Even if you'd gotten to drink that coffee, the cup would have been gone in ten minutes and so would the happiness. Then you'd be thinking about the *next* cup of coffee. We call it the hedonic treadmill—always searching for the next little happiness fix."

"What if somebody is holding a gun to my head?" I demanded, because this whole *just-be-happy-dammit* thing sounded a lot too Bobby McFerrin for a cynic like me.

"You don't have to be happy that the gun is there," Dr. Aymee conceded. "But you *can* feel compassion toward the person who is holding the gun, or you can think about how happy you *will* be when the gun is no longer there. Those choices are always available to you."

I thought about my current situation. I had a loving husband, healthy children, a beautiful house, a job I very much enjoyed, and enough money to take an occasional vacation. I was pretty damned happy. I tried to remember the last time I was sad or felt hopeless or even cried.

Oh yeah.

"Okay, my dad died nine years ago, and I miss him every

day," I heard myself telling her. "I suppose I could *choose* to focus on the fact that I had him at all, but I still can't think about him without getting angry and sad. Can you do anything about that?"

I actually started crying at this point. During an interview. You can imagine how professional I felt.

"Well," Dr. Aymee said with a little hesitation. *Ha!* I thought. *I've stumped her. She can't do it.* "I don't typically offer this," she continued, "but would you like to talk to your dad? Because I can do that."

"Shut the fuck up," I said, my whimpers turning to sobs. (Yes, I said *shut the fuck up* to a PhD during an interview in which I was sobbing. It really is too bad I work at home alone and can never be nominated for an employee of the month award.)

"I think you need to do this to be healed," Dr. Aymee said softly.

So I lit a candle and got a glass of water like she told me to do while she worked on getting my dad on the phone. The wait was interminable.

"Your dad wants you to talk to him more," she said finally. Which totally freaked me out because shortly after he died I had this crazy-real dream where he said to me, "I hear you talking about me, but I want you to talk *to* me," so I proceeded to drive around and talk to him where nobody could see or hear me, and if they did, they might think I just had an especially discreet wireless earpiece and wasn't in fact a *whack job driving aimlessly around town talking to her dead dad.*

"He wants you to get an angel statue to put on your desk and talk to him through that," she added. "A male angel."

Now I was sobbing and chatting with my dead dad through a doctor-cum-medium I'd never met and also Googling for angel statues. It's worth pointing out that my dad was the least religious person I have ever met, so I was definitely skeptical about his alleged request, but I figured maybe everyone gets a little holier after they die, so I kept scrolling.

"Did you find one yet?" Dr. Aymee wanted to know after a long silence occasionally punctuated by sniffles.

It turned out there were a shit-ton of male angel statues to choose from, but most of them were just . . . wrong. They were either too girly or garden-y or naked or holy-looking (Dad also liked the word *fuck* even more than I do). At one point, I stumbled across a shirtless black angel wearing what looked like white satiny genie pants, a gold belt, and wings twice the size of his lean but muscular body. There was a tiny black baby with Gary Coleman's *exact* face curled up at his feet. I couldn't help it; I laughed out loud when I saw it.

Now, Dr. Aymee couldn't see what I was looking at (shit, maybe she could!), and she couldn't have known how funny my dad was (or maybe she did!), but my cackle was all she needed to hear. "Your dad says you just found your angel," she told me.

$14.99 (plus shipping and handling) for a winged Batphone that goes exclusively to my dad? Of *course* I ordered it.

Black Angel (that's what my kids call him) now stands proudly on my desk, and I probably shouldn't admit this, but

I talk to him every day.* My daughters occasionally fight for the privilege of having him "sleep" by their beds, and the fact that they have never once questioned his presence or even suggested that a black baby-daddy statue was an odd thing to have on your desk cheers me up every time I think about it. I genuinely and honestly can talk about my dad now without feeling sad, which makes me believe that Dr. Aymee was right. We all can choose to be happier, even if we never win the lottery or get a raise or fit back into the jeans we wore in college. And if we decide not to be happier, statistics say it's going to happen anyway.

I'll drink to that.†

---

* I realize I should probably call him *African American Angel*, but I like to think that angels aren't concerned with race or country of origin.

† On the next non-weekday designated drinking night, of course.

Jenna McCarthy is an internationally published writer, former radio personality, and the author of a bunch of books for kids and adults. (Don't worry; her kids books are funny and sweet and don't have any swear words. She swears.) When she's not busy oversharing on Twitter, Facebook, and Instagram, she likes to troll Pinterest for crafts she'll never attempt and recipes she'll never make. She lives in ridiculously beautiful Santa Barbara, California, with her husband and two daughters, who sometimes even admit they are related to her. Visit her at jennamccarthy.com.